A SCAB
IS NO
SON OF MINE

A Scab
is no
Son of Mine

Stephen Whyles

To order additional copies of this book, contact:
Xlibris LLC
0-800-056-3182
www.xlibrispublishing.co.uk
Orders@xlibrispublishing.co.uk
670213

CONTENTS

Not Suitable reading for children

Profanity Warning

As one would expect with the Coal Mining Industry there is an awful
lot of severe foul language especially in the early chapters, Please do not
read this book if you are likely to be offended by reading profanity.
The use of profanity has been necessary to portray the
real life scenarios, events and feelings at the time.

Chapter 1

The Working Miner

There was a knock at the door, a knock that started my heart thumping, thumping more than it had ever thumped before. I knew that when I opened that door I would be opening the door to an uncertain world, an unfamiliar world, and a world filled with dread, anxiety and uncertainty. If I didn't answer the door, would the knock go away and life remain as it was, or would the knock continue, Could I just go back to bed?

No! I have to answer the door, I have been planning for this moment for the last six Months, but I didn't know just how scared I would actually be. I knew that from this moment on my life would change forever, no going back, no undoing the past, it's too late for that now, my mind is not so sure now.

My adopted family were behind me. What am I getting them into? What am I getting myself into? I made tentative steps towards the door, my feet felt like they had lead boots on them. I took a deep breath and opened the door. A Policeman stood proudly in front of my door.

He said "Stephen"?
(Me)   "*Yes*"
(Policeman) "Are you ready? we need to get you near the gate ready, the bus is a couple of minutes away"
(Me)   "Err. *Yes*."

He moved out of the way, I picked up my snap bag that my girlfriends mum had prepared for me. I looked down the garden path, I saw what seemed like dozens of policemen but I'm sure it was only a few. It was early dawn, the air was still, no bird song which I thought was strange for an early September morning, it was if the world was holding its breath in anticipation of what was about to take place. My stomach is in knots, I feel like I'm going to the gallows, and for all I know I could just be doing exactly that. This is the culmination of Months of turmoil and battling with my conscience.

A police van came over the bridge with armoured windscreen protection, closely followed by the bus, the bus I had been watching on the news for weeks. The police van pulled up just past the gate, and the bus pulled up at the gate, I took one look at the bus, it was armoured, with thick weld mesh encompassing it and covering all the windows, even the windscreen. One of the policemen put his hand my shoulder which made me jump, Jesus I'm like a cat on hot bricks, he said "right *son lets go*". My nerves are jangling big time, I even feel like I am going to throw up. The automatic door opened, oh my god the driver had a full face crash helmet on, there was another man stood at the front of the bus, he also had a full face crash helmet on. In his hand was a baseball bat. I thought my heart was thumping earlier, it's practically jumping out of my chest now. The driver's mate said "come *on lad get thi sen on*". I got on not needing to be told twice, you tend to take notice when someone tells you to do something with a baseball bat in his hand. I looked down the bus and saw about seven or eight other men sat in the seats quite spaced out rather than together. A voice piped up. "Well *done young Ian, thas dun rate thing, come and sit thi sen darn ere*". I sat down and the drivers mate came to me and said

"Well *done! That's not easy is it? Just one thing you need to know, if the bus gets overrun there are baseball bats in the racks above your head*". I now realised that this is not a scary as I thought it would be, it was a thousand times worse than that.

The bus set off on its way to the pit, I turned round to look at who else was on the bus, nobody I knew personally but I recognised all the faces. Some of them I had come across underground and some I had just seen around the pit top or in the baths. We were now drawn together compelled to whatever fate awaited us. By this time I had got my breath and said to the guy I sat with "*fuckin ell, I'm gonna throw up, that was pretty unnerving I weren't quite expecting that, in fact to be honest I didn't know what I was expecting, my legs are shaking like a dog avin a shit*" he and some of the others laughed, he said" *arr it gets easier but the woss bit is still to come*". Another guy came over he put his hand on my shoulder, he said, "*take no notice of him, he loves the adrenalin rush, it is frightening I can't say it int, the only preparation is to just do it, and it will get easier and you've got us now. The guys driving the bus are real hard cases nobody's gonna get past them in a hurry*".

In a strange way I did feel comforted by his words. He said "thar *Ian's lad aren't tha?*" I said "*yes, well at least A was until nar*"

He laughed and said "*look thas not done owt wrong, Yeah, ok, Ian is gonna be well pissed, but he's a commy and you can't reason wi them*"

I asked him what it was like for his first time, he said "*am not gonna pretend it wah easy, kin ell, it's never that even nar, but thar as to stand up foh what tha believes in and telling mi sen I'm doin rate thing, helps, I probably felt just the same as thar does nar, you will remember whats coming up in a few minutes foh rest o thi life I shouldn't wonder*"

He went back to his seat. I scanned the rest of the bus, they all had the same look on their face, I wouldn't say it was fear exactly but you could tell they weren't going to a holiday camp, that's for bloody sure. About then the drivers mate turned round and faced us all, and said "sounds *like it's a big turn out today*". That statement got my heart thumping again. I asked the guy next to me about a guy at the back of the bus, he looked more scared than me, and that was bloody saying something. He said *"yeah he's a fuckin coward, he's a bloody nervous wreck, he's only here cos their lass made him come back, she's one o them women that likes the good things in life and a bit of hardship is not her style, she stopped his tap and told him that she would leave him if he didn't come back to work and start bringing some money in"*.

I said" *bloody hell that must be a horrible situation to be in"*

He said *"well maybe it is, but the truth is he's a bloody coward, he should grow a pair and stand up to her, it's pathetic a bloody grown man like that shit scared of his misses"*.

I was thankful that I had a family that supported me 100%, albeit an adopted family. I was scared but I couldn't imagine what he was going through. I couldn't help but feel a little sorry for him and his situation. The fact that he was more on the side of the striking miners must have made his decision an impossible one.

My situation was different to the rest of them, there were father and sons together that had gone back, the rest were married men, with supporting wives back home. I had to leave my home and be estranged from my dad. He made it clear that I wouldn't be welcome in his house if I returned to work. My choice was an easy hard one if that makes sense, I was dead set against the strike moreover the lack of a national ballot. My dad just refused point blank to hear my opinion, not even an agree to differ. He told me at the time that I would have to live with that decision for the rest of my life and that there were miners in the village that went back to work in the 1926 strike and they are stilled called a scab. Nevertheless the easy part was that my dad was willing to disown me for doing something legal, whilst he was doing something illegal, the strike had been ruled illegal due to the refusal by Arthur Scargill to call a national ballot. All through my childhood all he drilled into us was to not bring any trouble or more importantly police to the door. That enraged me, obviously blood is not thicker than water in his eyes. How could he disown me over a political opinion? Ok I could see that my going back to work would be embarrassing for him, but bloody hell I am his son.

By now the bus had turned onto Southfield lane, it's just a couple of minutes now from the pit. There is a humped railway bridge about a quarter of a mile before the pit entrance, once you get to the top of that bridge you can see all the pit. The drivers mate turned again and said *"ere we goo agen"*.

My heart was well and truly pounding, my head was all over the place, lots of questions, and like what is this going to be like will it be as bad as or worse than I had seen on the TV? Will I see my dad on the picket line? Will he see me? Will the bus be bombarded with missiles as I had also seen on the TV? Well whatever the questions they were about to be answered in the next thirty seconds or so.

The bus mounted the bridge, I was eager to see how many pickets there was. I looked and instantly the silence broke and there was hundreds literally hundreds of pickets lining both sides of the road, the noise was deafening, it was like a scene from a war film, there was a strong police line in front of the pickets on both sides of the road all linked arm in arm, the pickets were pushing at the lines to try and get to the bus. How the hell they held all them back was nothing short of amazing. The noise was horrendous, the abuse being hurled was something else, *"joooooodas, scaaaaaaaaabs,"* were just some of what could be picked out from the melee. This lasted for what seemed like an eternity, the guy next to me said *"just listen to the fuckin idiots, every day the same, fuckin pathetic"*. I though ohhhh myyyyy goddddd, this is it now every day, the same. I knew I was doing the right thing but that doesn't make this experience any the less frightening. The fact of the matter is everybody on that bus was going through the same mixed emotions that I was. We were together but separate in a way, each with his own emotions and way of dealing with the situation. Whatever your way of handling it, it would not be easy. It was akin to the scenes you see on the TV when a child killer or serial rapist is being driven to court and there is an angry mob of people pushing and shoving the police to get to the police van. Only difference is we were not child killers or serial rapists, we were just a group of mine workers upholding our fundamental right to go to work. We are in a bus, a bus that is armoured, we had a police escort in front and behind. The experience that we just endured was horrific. The mob pushing to get at us was totalling a fair few hundred not just a dozen or so. In that regard we felt worse than a convicted killer because the scenes outside were similar to the scenes mentioned earlier but on a much grander scale. I had agonised over this decision for Months, as soon as Scargill was spouting on the TV that there was no need for a national ballot, I knew I would have to do something about it. The scenes on the TV showing police and strikers with blood streaming down their faces only served to emphasise how bitter this dispute was, I had never seen anything like it before. It is without doubt a civil war a civil war where there was no middle ground, you were either on the side of Scargill or the side of the government. The fact is these men that were on the bus with me were not on either side, myself included. We were on the side of democracy. Everybody on this bus would be out on strike if there was a national ballot and if the vote was for strike action. I knew therefore that there was no mandate for a strike, there wasn't even a will for strike at the beginning. It was easy to have your view of right and wrong, it was quite another to act upon it, given what the consequences of doing so would be. I felt ashamed to a small degree that I had let intimidation keep me out of the pit for six Months.

The bus turned swiftly into the pit yard, this was well practised, I could tell that. The drivers mate turned round and said" that *woh dissapointin, where woh fuckin bricks?" not one fucker hit the bus, arr they must be running art on steam be nar"*.

In a way I can understand the betrayal that the pickets were feeling, after all the working environment underground meant that you had to have a strong bond and a sense of trust, your life depended very much on the man next to you watching your back and vice versa. The camaraderie was strong it had to be the pit couldn't function without it. You had to work together as one. It was a brotherhood in a way. It was a way of life rather than just a job. The saying that Mineworkers are born and bred as miners is very true. A miner's son was destined to follow his dad down the mine. I always had a sense of belonging, well, at least up to now that is. No one knows how this is going to end. Whatever the end would be one thing I was certain of was that the pit would never be the same again, the working relationship would never be the same again. Life it's self will never be the same again!

I have made my bed as it were and now I have to lie in it. There is no going back now, the deed is done and cannot be undone.

One of the guys came over and said "Well, young Ian, how's tha feel nar"? (Me) "Well to be honest I'm kinda ok nar, that wah fuckin unbelievable, but I'm glad I done it". (Miner) "Yeah thar a young kid but a young kid wi balls, and thi faather well, fuck him, he dunt deserve to ave a kid like thee".

CHAPTER 2

The Early Years

I was born in December of 1962. I lived in a very modest terraced house locally known as pit row, in fact the name of the terraces was called Colliery row. I lived here with my Mother and Father two brothers and a sister, a dog and a cat. All residents of colliery row had a father or husband that worked at the pit. To quote an old cliché it was a very close knit community, never locking doors when nipping out to the shops, neighbours just knocking and walking in for a cuppa and a gossip. Of course we all had one thing in common and that of course was the coal mine.

I can still picture the image standing at the end of our yard looking down at the pit tip with the headstocks clearly prominent, always expecting that one day I would be heading down there and following my father down the mine. I was oblivious then to the radical change in my life that the pit would bring.

My early childhood was much like any other within the coal mining community, we played as children in and around the terraced houses and playing the games of the day such as hot rice, Blind man's bluff, Tin can a larky, to name just a few. Of course in those days there was no video games or Internet to entertain us, and only 3 channels on the black and white TV. We enjoyed all of those purely because we didn't know anything else, but it was a largely happy time for us as children.

The family routine was the same day in and day out, a little bit like Groundhog Day. When Dad was on the night shift I would be sent to wake him up at 7 o'clock whilst my Mother was cooking his supper, funny thing was it always seemed to be kippers or bacon egg and beans. He would get up some minutes after and eat his supper then toddle off to the pit, we would wake up the following morning and he would be in bed, I can tell you it took me a while to figure that one out. The same pattern would be repeated for the other two shifts the only difference being the time of day.

Money was always tight but my Mother always seemed to find plenty for the local working men's club where she played her beloved bingo.

As for holidays, they were few and far between. If we were lucky enough to go on holiday it was to my Aunty Sue's house in Weston super mare, rather a very large bungalow. Aunt Sue being my Mother's Sister had taken a different path with the exception of marrying a coal miner from a different pit. Her Husband (*Uncle Stuart*) was an electrician down the pit, but soon left to find his fortune as a self-employed electrician, judging by the size of his property, land, and his love of Rolls Royce motor cars he was very successful. Even at an early age the differences between him and my dad were plain to see, my dad often spoke with a little resentment when referring to him. I know now that was more to do with politics than wealth. Uncle Stuart would visit occasionally and be driving one of his beloved Rolls Royce cars, this caused great interest with the local kids, after-all one would hardly expect to see a Rolls Royce parked outside a terrace house on Colliery row. I recall as a young boy being very proud that we had a rich relative. The only other holiday that we were assured of (*if one can call it a holiday*) was the annual day trip to Cleethorpes, arranged by the local working men's club.

The village was supported predominantly by the coal miners and their families, sure, there were other businesses within the village most notably the dolomite quarry, but the pit was by far the largest employer employing nearly 1000 men most of whom came from Whitwell.

The only downside I could see to this community was that everybody knew everybody else's business, this meant that whatever we did as kids, and where ever we did it, everybody knew about it, and of course, that meant that it got back to our parents.

My childhood memories are mixed when it comes to my parents. I knew there was no doubt what-so-ever that I was loved by my dad. However; the same could not be said for my Mother. There are very early experiences and painful memories of my mother that quite frankly, I find difficult to put into words here, needless to say they were far from happy ones. One notable and painful memory I have is having a slice of dry bread being thrown to me on the toilet floor that was my breakfast, my older brother who would have been about nine years old remembers that to this very day and he's fifty five now.

I think I speak for my siblings too when I say my father was by and large approachable, we were scared to disobey him although he never once laid a finger on us, a raised voice was more than enough to bring us into line. But never the less we never pushed it, we knew were the uncrossable line was drawn. He was respected within the community and his peers always spoke well of him. I was constantly referred to as "Ian's lad". In a funny sort of way that made me feel proud, not so much for me, but that my father was well liked in the community.

From my point of view as a young boy my father's life consisted of bed and work, and very little else, he occasionally liked to play golf and pursued this with his friends, some of whom were not in the coal mining industry but did have connections with it. He was a caring man in a lot of ways, we could pretty much do what we wanted so long as we didn't bring any trouble home, from what I remember that was his only demand of us, well; after our chores that is!

My father was a very political man, he was, and still is, a very staunch supporter of Marxism. His views were very extreme to some but were by and large in line with his fellow miners. Now I fully understand where the resentment with my Uncle Stuart came from, as Uncle Stuart is a conservative supporter, or Tory, as he was commonly called. Politically they couldn't be any further apart but were compelled to get along due to the relationship. I.e. being brother's in law.

In his spare time he would be either watching cricket or football on the TV, or reading. He could often be seen with a bundle of the Militant newspaper, where he was selling them to help fund the Marxist movement. He was an educated man for a miner, having good grades and a levels from the grammar school. Yet, I feel that he wasted these down the mine never having any ambitions, and was content to be a coal hewer for the majority of his 30 odd years down the pit. From what I can tell, his far left political views prevented him from doing what most of us today aspire to, that being, owning our own home and trying to create wealth. My father viewed this as capitalism and that was a big no no as far as he was concerned. My relationship with my father will be covered in greater detail later in this book.

As stated earlier in this chapter my relationship with my Mother was something else entirely, also as stated earlier some experiences and memories will be skipped and I will concentrate on my Mother away from that where possible.

From my very earliest memories I always knew that I was different from my siblings when it came to the way we were treated by my Mother. To this day I don't know why that was, it was clear to me that she resented me for some reason. I cannot recall any single occasion where she showed any love at all, I always feared her and watched my back constantly. More worryingly I dreaded being alone with her, she was always vicious at worst and stand offish at best especially when my father was not around. I'm not sure to this day whether or not he was aware of this, but I find it hard that anyone could not notice, my friends certainly noticed it and it was often brought up when playing out. I spent every waking moment playing out whether it was rain, snow or blow. This was the only way I could relax and enjoy life without constantly looking over my shoulder. To avoid straying into vivid detail I will refrain from this part of my Mother. I found the titbits I have mentioned so far very difficult to recall, let alone write. The only good thing about my Mother as I see it was that I was fed and clothed and watered. My Grandmother (on my father's side) however loved me very much and never missed an opportunity to show it. My Mother and Grandmother never really got on as we were growing up. Every Sunday I and my older Brother and my dad would go to Grandma's house for Sunday lunch but my mother never ever went. My younger Brother and Sister weren't born then. In later years my Grandma told me a few things she knew about me and my Mothers relationship, It was clear that she was more than aware of my mother's resentment towards me, although we never discussed it in detail. I always felt like I was my Grandmothers favourite and maybe that could be down to the way my mother was with me. Needless to say as soon as I was able I left home and moved into a dingy bedsit in Worksop, but believe me, this was heaven. Compared to the life at home.

My secondary schooling was at Boughton Lane comprehensive school in Clowne although initially it was a secondary school. Many of my fellow pupils were miner's sons and daughters though not all. My school days were by and large happy days. I remember though one day being asked to stay behind after a Geography class to see the teacher. When the other pupils had left the classroom the teacher asked me if everything was alright at home, I said "yes sir, why?" he said that some of the teachers had noticed that I was sometimes staring into space and not concentrating on the lessons. I remember shockingly how he was saying that he suspected that all was not well and that it was ok to talk to him about anything, and that if I ever felt that I could not go home, I was to tell him immediately. I guess the teachers were more intelligent than I gave them credit for. I very nearly told him but felt that something was wrong with me and that it was my fault, and more importantly I didn't want all my friends and other pupils to laugh at me and make fun of me, silly I know, but, it was the way I felt. My feelings today about my Mother are filled with bitterness, anger, resentment and emptiness, no other emotions at all. It's very difficult to refer to my Mother without the anger and bitterness showing, but I guess I have said enough for you to get the gist.

Outside of school I spent my free time from twelve years old and onwards over at Frank Birds. Frank was the local market gardener who grew roses, dahlias, scabius, sweet Williams and other flowers, as younger kids he would often tell us off for jumping the fence into his flower beds to retrieve our balls that had gone over there, whether they be cricket or footballs, they all ended up going over the fence, in our cricket games if we hit the ball over the fence it was classed as six and out, and of course we had to fetch the ball back.

I cannot remember how it started apart from me standing at the fence watching him ploughing the fields with his tractor, He invited me over the fence and I rode on the back of his tractor. Trust me I was in seventh heaven. Frank was a devout Christian and attended church every Sunday without fail, and yes he had connections with the coal mines, he had spent twenty years of his life working down Whitwell pit. As the years went by I spent every waking moment out of school with him in the fields, he taught me to drive the tractor and to use the cultivator and plough, by the time I was fourteen I was ploughing his fields for him on my own.

I always felt privileged being allowed by Frank to spend all my time with him, he was a kind gentle god fearing man and I sensed he had a soft spot for me, I respected and admired him greatly and could never do enough for him, he had a twin brother Ernest, Ernest had suffered all his life with epilepsy and Frank had forgone his own life to look after him, Ernest was not however a church goer, in fact far from it, he was feared by all of us kids, If he caught us in the field retrieving our ball he would call the police because of the damage we were doing to the plants, we always strode between the furrows of plants but inevitably some plants did get damaged. As the years went by however I got to know Ernest and found him to be far from the ogre we thought he was and was in fact a down to earth guy, I would often go up to Franks house for lunch whilst working in his field, and yes if I called round outside of these times I would just knock and walk in, that was the norm in those days. Ernest as I said earlier suffered from birth with epilepsy and as a result missed most of his schooling. Ultimately this resulted in him being illiterate, Frank promised his mother that he would look after Ernest and gave up happiness with his best friend's sister to stay and look after Ern. To that end Frank and Ernest lived together all their lives. Frank and Ern were totally different. In the many years that I had spent with them I never once heard Frank swear. In fact people have told me that he never swore when he worked down the pit, which believe me is remarkable if not nigh on impossible. Whilst Ernest did swear it was very very mild, never once using what was commonly known as Pit talk. I found it remarkable that whilst Ern was illiterate he could knock a good tune out of the piano that they had. Needless to say these were the good times for me and I often look back on them with fondness.

CHAPTER 3

The School Years

It is said that the school days are the best days of your life. I never really believed this statement whilst I was at school, and to a certain degree I don't believe it now. However; I have often said that I wished I knew then what I know now, but I guess that statement is true in most of us. I did to some extent enjoy my school years, it was an escape from my life at home and I did make a lot of friends there.

It was in Whitwell junior school where I first realised that politics would shape my future, there was one particular teacher there, Mrs. Sternberg, Her son was connected in some way with the conservative party, I think he may have been an MP. Mrs. Sternberg was very hostile to me, I was always the butt of her sarcasm and I always seemed to be making trips to the head master's office on her say so. If there was ever a problem, which there often was, like fighting or being out of bounds, if I was there I was the culprit in her eyes and I was the one being sent to the head master to explain myself. It was only in later years that I realised that there were often conflicts between her and my dad politically, and obviously she took out her frustrations out on me to get back at him. That is the only way I can explain her behaviour, I often finished up getting the slipper from the headmaster purely on her say so.

There were people I had a liking for, most notably April Shaw, she lived across the road from colliery row and her father was self-employed. Their

---

house was large by anyone's standards and stood in its own grounds. It also had a very nice orchard with big tempting juicy pears, there's always a down side and that was the very large pair of Alsatian dogs, the bark alone shook the ground, scrumping from that orchard would have been a suicide mission. April is the same age as me and was no way connected with the coal mine, Mervin her father however worked at Whitwell pit and worked his way up to being a deputy before leaving in the mid 60's. My association with April really came about by my association with Frank Bird. I know her and her father used to come round to franks field to chat with Frank. It was really around that time that I got to know April, we spent some time round her house playing in her numerous outbuildings. Mervin her father was a very welcoming man as I recall and always smiling, it was clear from the outset that the love between April and her father was very enviable.

In 1977 the residents of colliery row held a street party to celebrate the queen's silver jubilee, I still to this day find that strange because miners that I knew tended to be anti-royalist, my father certainly was and played no part in the celebrations, April however; played her accordion at the occasion and this went down very well. April I know never knew just how talented she was.

One of my closest friends as a small boy was Steve Cooling, to this day we remain close. Steve lived on colliery row and before I started spending most of my time at Franks, we played together all the time, even after going to Franks Steve would sometimes come round with me. Steve's father was also a miner at Whitwell pit.

Another close friend was Kevin Wholstenholme he lived next door to me and his dad again worked at the pit as an electrician. Kevin also spent a lot of time at Franks and was a favourite of Frank's, Frank would often ask me where he was when I went round there. Once we started secondary school Kevin drifted away from both me and Frank, presumably because he had made new friends.

The older I became the longer I would stay away from home, becoming very much a loner to some degree. I spent more and more time round at Franks. One particular aspect of being with Frank that I particularly enjoyed was helping him collect moss for his wreaths, Frank did flowers and wreaths for weddings and funerals in the village, we used to drive off to the private estates in nearby Welbeck and clumber. Frank had special access to areas that weren't accessible to the public, and this gave me a good opportunity to see birds and animals that one would not normally see due to the isolated nature of the area we were in. One of my passions was bird watching and I indulged in this hobby at every opportunity. I would often be up at the crack of dawn during school holidays and go bird watching in Whitwell wood or the woods down broad lane. This hobby is hardly a group activity and fitted in with my need to be alone.

I was also a fan of country music and enjoyed listening to tapes of Johnny Cash, Jim Reeves and the like, all my school friends were listening to the pop music of the day, most would find it strange that I liked country music, it was clear that the older I got the more alienated from my school mates I became merely through liking different things which meant we had very little in common other than the school. My school mates were keen on football and rugby, in summer it was cricket and athletics, I detested all of these and had no interest in sport at all, other than motor racing, luckily my dad tolerated motor racing so I was able to watch this on TV during the summer season. Don't get me wrong I wasn't totally alienated from school mates, I did share the same taste in TV programmes with the exception of top of the pops that is.

School lessons were enjoyable to some degree, I particularly enjoyed English, history and geography. I was unable to ever grasp maths and was totally out of touch when it came to that, the down side there was I was unable to take part in physics as I had an interest in that but was unable to take physics because one had to be good at maths to be accepted. I was however able to take the electrical installations course at the local college and was regularly near the top of the class with that, little knowing that would shape my career later in my life.

Like all kids puberty soon fell upon us, I was no different to them there. A lot of my friends were quick to acquire boyfriends and girlfriends, I however was a little slower in that department. The earliest encounter with girls was with a girl called Anne Bradley she was in my class and seemed to have an interest in me that made me feel uneasy, however; I accepted an invitation to go to her house for tea after school, she lived in barlborough and that was only a few minutes bus ride away. She was into judo and was very keen to show me her moves with me being her practice dummy. We had tea and was surprised that she made the tea and that her Mother was not at home, her Mother was a single parent and worked. When I got home my dad asked me how I got on with Anne, I was a little defensive and not to mention embarrassed, but it turned out that he knew her mother as she was connected with him and his political activities so I felt the whole thing had been pre-planned. It wasn't long however before I got the bug and was pretty forward in trying to get involved with girls at a sexual level. I failed quite often in that area but there were a few conquests, I was proud to have lost my virginity at 14, little realising that this was a lot later than my peers.

I always considered myself to be from the poorer end of the scale compared to other pupils of my year, however; I soon realised that I was not amongst the poorest. There were plenty of pupils there far less fortunate than me. There were a few kids that were on free school meals, obviously this was an indicator of the social standing of the person concerned. Free school meals were a brilliant idea mainly because it ensured that everybody had at least one cooked meal per day during the week, however; from the kids point of view it did highlight that they were poor and in that regard it was a little cruel. I remember thinking that people that paid for their meals should pay at reception rather than being called out to the front of class. That way although the kids who were on free meals were not highlighted by teachers and staff, the very fact that their names were not called out did in fact highlight that fact to their peers. Unfortunately I did witness some teasing of people who were on free school meals. I did pay for meals and readily handed over £1.25p per week.

Dress code was standard and was designed to make everybody look the same so as not to alienate poorer kids, but that failed too in some ways, some kids came into school with dirty clothes and dirt picked up on skin during games periods like football and rugby were still visible days later. I had many friends at school and from all backgrounds, I am proud today that I did not alienate people just because of their social standing.

In many ways I was a typical school pupil no different to the next pupil really, I was fortunate that I was not subject to bullying and proud that I was not responsible for it either. Bullying did take place and I suppose that's a downside to putting lots of kids together, attitudes were different then than they are today and I know that the poor kids that were subject to bullying suffered in silence.

Discipline at school was quite widespread, corporal punishment was very much prevalent and I did witness pupils being caned or slippered in class. Many people had opinions on that but no matter what ones opinion might be one only has to look at kids attitudes today compared to then, for example as a kid in school in the 70's one would not dare to answer the teacher back and be disrespectful, unlike today. So considering my early childhood at the hands of my Mother one would expect me to be against all forms of discipline. The truth is discipline is one thing whatever your views, abuse is quite another and different entirely. But my last word on that is people of that era had a lot more respect for their elders than they do today and personally I feel that is directly as a result of the abolition of school discipline.

Towards the end of secondary schooling the emphasis was for our future careers, in the third year we had to pick the subjects that would be helpful in our career choice, I remember great emphasis at the time on the importance of choosing wisely, I was in the non-exam groups of the core subjects like Maths and English. I knew this would be important but I always expected to be following my father down the coal mine, During the 1972 miners' strike I vividly remember the chants on the picket lines, most notably "A job for my son's and my son's son's". I remember my dad asking me what subjects I had chosen and whether I had any idea what I wanted to do once I left school, I told him that I was going down the pit. I was shocked when he then said that no son of mine is going down the pit, when you are eighteen you can please yourself. I reminded him then of the chants on the picket lines., but I was told in no uncertain terms not to answer back. A few kids at school had parents that had their own businesses and they would naturally be part of that, I now however knew that I would not be going down the pit at least until I was eighteen, so I had two years that I would have to find something else. During careers interviews at school I discussed my options with the careers advisor, it seemed that the only option for me was farming as I was experienced in that regard through driving Frankie Birds tractor.

It was about this time that I discovered cigarettes and would often be found at the back of the technical drawing terrapins smoking with my peers. One teacher (who will remain nameless) even turned a blind eye to smoking in class. I can happily say that drugs and drug abuse was something that was not prevalent then and I never heard of anyone who was addicted to drugs, in fact, I don't honestly think it was widespread at all unlike today. Drinking however; was prevalent and I know of some kids that had alcohol in school, no surprise really, I know that I was able to purchase a pint of mild or bitter in one pub in the village at just 14 years old, and I was by no means the only one either. My father was not a drinker or at least we never witnessed him drinking or even going to the pub for that matter. My Mother was indeed a drinker but only drank in the middle club and never in the pub I used to sneak into, so there was little chance of being caught. It was not until I was in my late 40's that I discovered that my father did drink and used to race to the middle club after he had finished the afternoon shift to get there in time for last orders. My Mother drank constantly, or so it seemed, she would often have a beer in a mug presumably to mask the fact it was beer, because we did have drinking glasses. Both my Mother and Father were smokers, so it would be easy to think that was where I got it from, but to be honest, none of my Brothers or Sister have ever smoked even to this day so that was not the reason I was smoking.

I can vividly remember being sat at home one night after school watching TV, it would be early evening and my older brother was looking after us as my Mother was in the middle club. When there was a knock at the door and a man walking in dressed in coal miners attire, he asked where my Mother was and my brother told him that she was in the club, It later transpired that my dad had suffered a heart attack underground and had been rushed to hospital, it was a scary experience for me. Shamefully and selfishly I can remember thinking that if he died life would be unbearable for me with just my Mother. Thankfully though not just for personal reasons either he did recover from that, or he has never touched another cigarette since then.

As I said earlier most of my childhood was spent round at Frankie Birds either on my own or with my best friend Steve Cooling, being on a market garden nursery that had over 7 acres was a good place to spend time, I was taught at an early age how to shoot a double barrelled shot gun, I thoroughly enjoyed this pastime and could often be seen on Franks fields with the various friends that Frank had, who just happened to have shot guns, rabbitting, this was a great pastime for me spending a lot of the evenings or early mornings on the fields or railway bankings rabbitting. I had guns of my own but not shot guns, I had a 2.2 high powered air rifle with telescopic scope, and this rifle to give you some idea could easily kill a rabbit over quarter a mile away. The other gun I had was at the other end of the scale and was an affectionally known as a pop out pistol, this pistol was 1.77 bore and had a range of about 20 feet. Me and Steve used to fool around with this gun quite often as it was relatively safe, except that is in the hands of an idiot, every village has its idiot and that was me, one day whilst playing, Steve said

"I bet you couldn't shoot me with that thing".

Always up for a challenge I said

"Ok you're on, start running".

He soon set off running up the field dancing from left to right as he ran, I aimed the pistol straight down the middle of his zig zagging and pulled the trigger, well he dropped like a sack of poop, the pellet taking him out from his ankle. Funny as hell now but really idiotic. All sense and reason went out of the window when we were together.

Good friends however are hard to come by and Steve was a good friend and we remain good friends to this day. Friends stick together through thick and thin and I and Steve have certainly done that.

Everybody has a story to tell about their childhood I suppose, mine was perhaps not too different from most, when I recollect my early years I always seem to be alone, well from parental company at least, Dad was happy for us to do our own thing provided we didn't bring any trouble home, my Mother. Well let's just say my being out of the house all day was to a mutual benefit.

CHAPTER 4

Venturing into the world of work

My dad had strong political beliefs and could often be found selling the Militant newspaper either at the pit or in Worksop town centre. It was about this time that I took a vague interest in politics, I grew up with my dad's left wing views but at the time I was easily influenced, Every boy wants his dad to be proud of him, My dad spoke to me about setting up a young socialists group and wanted me to be the chairman, I agreed and was soon writing my first political statement with my dad's heavy influence. An inaugural meeting was arranged in the rooms above holmefield arms, it was a publicity exercise and the turnout was overwhelming. I was sat at the front alongside my dad, Dennis Skinner and another trade union activist I believe his name was Brian Mcguigan but I am not absolutely sure. So we started the meeting and very soon I was reading the speech that me and my dad had written, pretty disconcerting really because as I was reading it I was thinking that it didn't reflect what I believed. It wasn't until Dennis Skinner started spouting off that I realised that I was in the wrong place. The overriding thing that nailed it for me was when my dad was going on about the unemployment figures which were around 2.5 million and he was saying that if there were no jobs then jobseekers should be paid a full time wage. The answer to that statement came into my head like a seven pound sledge hammer, I was thinking if that was the case where was the incentive to find work and more importantly who would pay for that. My dad's answer no doubt would have been to tax the rich heavily. Of course statements like that would appeal to the unemployed and to people who resented the rich and wealthy. My views were that although a small number of people are born into wealthy households the vast majority were rich or wealthy through their own hard work, after all no one becomes rich waiting for or relying on state hand-outs. If you want the good things in life you have to work for it. I know Mining villages were generally poor but that was not the fault of the rich and wealthy people. I accepted that there was a class society that existed at the time but there was no rule or law that prevented one from climbing out of poverty, it's a matter of application surely. Easier said than done I know and I also knew that particular view would have been in the minority. So it was now clear to me that I was going to clash with my dad politically unless of course I adopted his point of view. Little did I realise that in a few years' time this clash was going to come to ahead with Dior consequences'.

So I left school and I secured a job at a farm near Van Dykes, I had to walk it there from Colliery row which was a good 2 mile. Start time was 5am, which was a killer. Getting up at stupid o'clock was a killer, not finishing until 7:30pm meant for a hell of a long day and a long walk back afterwards, needless to say I soon left that job.

My next job was at the paper factory in Whitwell, this was an interesting job apart from baling cardboard that is, being a lorry drivers mate was great, driving round the midlands collecting cardboard for baling and recycling. We came home most days with various goods from records to sweets, the factory was located opposite Whitwell signal box and stood alongside the railway line, I spent many a lunch time in the signal box. This job was getting me nearer to the pit in both location and direction.

Fig00 Whitwell paper factory
Picture courtesy of and dedicated to Mr G Bennett

Soon after starting this Job I decided to move into a dingy bedsit in Worksop, on Park Street to be exact. I stayed here for 8 Months until it was closed down by the health inspector. I was unable to find another one so had no choice but to go back home, this arrangement suited neither me or my Mother. In that short time my bed had been got rid of so had to sleep on the floor on cushions in the attic, beggars can't be choosers I suppose. I got another job in the village as a labourer for a local builder in High Street, I enjoyed this job too, hard work mind but enjoyable nonetheless. I had some good times here meeting lots of different people not to mention girls. The job as a labourer lasted a couple of years but they were a good couple of years.

I was now over 18 years old so I told my dad that I wanted to go to the pit as jobs now were very scarce, especially for someone that left school with no formal qualifications, my dad agreed to help me get on the waiting list and it wasn't long before I had an interview with the personnel manager at Whitwell pit. I remember him vividly he was such an obnoxious and sarcastic sod, he was a boss hog look alike without the white suit. Trying his utmost to scare me off and to try to wind me up by making comments about my dad. Luckily I didn't rise to it.

Well I was soon offered a position and was soon winging my way to Williamthorpe colliery for training. This was exciting, in a funny peculiar way it seemed as though I had reached my destiny and following in my dad's footsteps, I suppose you could say I was a man at last. I had no incline what so ever then that this job would change my life and direction in lots of ways, mostly negative ones.

I had my full medical and that was the only time I would ever let another man touch my nuts without chinning him. The phrase I believe he used was "cough and drop".

My trainer at Williamthorpe was a guy known as tiny, he was one of my dad's mates, I thought my passage here would be easy, well I got that wrong, but I loved it nonetheless. I remember going down the shaft for the very first time, it was exciting, two of the lads that was with us refused to get in the cage so it was just the four of us and of course tiny. Even if I was scared I wouldn't have been able to back out as it would have impacted on my dad, but luckily I loved it. I remember thinking that I would probably have to drop to my knees once getting out of the cage, this was the impression I had at that time, all images of underground life seemed to be of miners crawling on their knees. I was astounded when the cage reached the inset level and we got off the ceiling was at least 15 foot above us. The air was kind of foul and fusty and everything was covered in stone dust which was used to keep the dust layers down.

We spent the first few days learning how to stop runaway trams, how to use a self-rescuer in simulated fire conditions. The firefighting training was something else, when we did the water hose training it took two of us all we had to stop it slapping us all over the yard, the pressure was unbelievable. I remember Tiny saying that if a fire required two hoses it was known as the Spanish situation and required hose A and hose B, it took me a long while to get that joke as I was the only one with the confused look on my face thinking what the hell have I just missed. The penny dropped eventually.

Next it was back on the surface for shovel practice, Jesus the shovel they gave us looked like a stick with the jodrell bank radio telescope dish on the end of it. I wasn't sure I would be able to lift the bloody thing empty let alone full of coal. Anyhow training went on for a few weeks, practicing escape techniques in smoke filled tunnels to simulate a fire underground, learning how to attach the self-rescuer in the dark. The self-rescuer or SCSR to give it its full title (Self Contained Self Rescuer) was an aluminium canister which contained a chemical oxygen generator designed to provide an air supply for a maximum of ninety minutes.

Another danger underground was the ever present gas, the two types of gas we were trained for was Black damp and fire damp. Black damp was a colourless, odourless and invisible gas. The feature of this gas was that it was heavier than air so resided within a couple of feet from the ground, which meant that if you was to sit on the floor to eat your snap then you ran the risk of being rendered unconscious and if not found quickly you would die!. I can tell you that gets your attention!, you're hardly likely to forget that sort of training if by doing so would kill you. Of course the gas wasn't constantly there and it was monitored.

The second gas was known as fire damp and in lay man's terms was much like household gas which became explosive at around 5%. Needless to say sparks were a hazard, to eliminate the risk of explosion all machinery was intrinsically safe which basically meant that if the machine failed no sparks would escape beyond the confines of the machine housing. All miners were subject to contraband searches before going underground for smoking materials mostly but for any other items that could cause a spark. You could be forgiven for thinking that we wouldn't need searching as common sense would stop you taking smoking materials underground but believe me it had been known. I have smelled cigarette smoke underground on a couple of occasions. To understand the layout of the mine somewhat, I will try to give a basic idea, the mine consisted of two shafts, number 1 and number 2, number 1 shaft was the mineral winding shaft and was also the air intake shaft, number 2 shaft was the man riding shaft but was used occasionally for equipment transportation. The air was drawn into the mine at the number 1 shaft and was drawn through all the roadways (*tunnels*) and then drawn out as stale air through number 2 shaft. On the rare occasion that cigarette smoke was smelled it was always at the number 1 shaft area, I believe it was in the old stables area at the back of the shaft. When ponies were in use in the mine they were stabled here.

By far and above any dangers in the mine roof falls were the most feared and most likely, a lot of geological tests were carried out by surveyors and the like but it was always a clear and present danger. This danger was most apparent at the road heading area, this is where the roadways were advanced along with the coal face, rings (*steel archways*) were set every metre or so to support the roof. As part of our basic training we spent some time down Bolsover colliery. By far the most scary and exciting was the trip down the coal face, this is where the most action is and by far the most dangerous, I remember being shocked at how little head room there was, and the noise was something else. You couldn't hear yourself think let alone talk.

Fig 2
This picture is of Whitwell Colliery in the eighties prior to closing.
Picture courtesy of Phil Sangwell

Fig 3
This picture is of Whitwell Colliery in the 60's
Picture courtesy of nottsexminer

We began by crawling along the face in between the roof masters, these roof masters are constantly inching forward and advancing with the coal face, not a place for the faint hearted.

One thing we learned very quickly is the camaraderie amongst coal miners, this is not hard to imagine as we all depended on each other for each other's safety. It was very evident that you had to have your wits about you when underground so to have someone watching your back too was comforting.

After our underground visit at Bolsover we headed towards the pit bottom for the trip back up to the surface. Whilst awaiting for the cage there were a few collier's *(face workers)* waiting also. This is where we witnessed our first taste of teasing and a better understanding of what is commonly known as pit talk, in other words foul language. Although the teasing and ribbing was quite intimidating it had no malicious intent.

We were soon to be on the cage riding to the surface, the cage was a double Decker as most are, with twelve men on the top deck and twelve men on the bottom deck. Next to come was our first experience of the pit baths, this is no place for anybody that is shy about getting undressed in front of other people, we all stripped off and went into the communal showers, Tiny our trainer told us that in here it was not uncommon for miners to scrub each other's back's. So far from just watching each other's back's they actually scrubbed them too. Pit baths at some collieries were a luxury that came in the late sixties, early seventies and were the result of tireless campaigning by the miners and the unions. Once training was completed it was back to Whitwell colliery to start work underground, form the first few weeks we were under CPS (close personal supervision). This is where you are assigned to a mentor, disappointingly we had to start work on the surface working on the various aspects of coal prep on the surface. My first few weeks were spent working on the screens, this is where the coal is sorted into its various sizes. The coal was emptied from the shaft at the surface directly onto the plate belt which then was transported via another belt into a large mobile hopper ready for feeding into the screens. The first machine the coal encountered was the shaker or shecker as we called it, this was just a glorified sieve system that shook the coal and sieved it through various sized holes. All the slack was transported via another belt to the transport area ready for shipping to the pit tip. The rest of the coal came from off the end of the shecker onto another belt where an operative would be standing. My mentor was on this position so I had to join him. The job was for us to remove any foreign objects that passed us such as wood etc., basically anything that wasn't coal, the culture shock here was that everything was the same colour i.e. black and sometimes we would grasp something that was obviously not coal and it would turn out to be human excrement. No detailed explanation needed here, suffice to say that there are no toilets underground so the belts were often used to serve that purpose as it would remove the waste away from confined working areas. The downside was it would often be picked up (literally) on the screens. After the coal passed us the coal was then dropped into a sizing machine, basically a hopper with two rollers that had picks attached and set to the required size. Everything that dropped into here would be crushed to the required size, whether that be coal wood or flesh and bones. Over the top of the Sizer was a giant electro magnet this was to pick out any metal objects especially tools. Occasionally the Sizer would get clogged and it had to be cleaned out manually, the safety process here was that the pummel had to be disconnected before entering the Sizer obviously if it were to start up with someone in there you would be mincemeat in seconds. The pummel is quite simply an industrial plug that plugs into the power supply. After this process the coal would then go up to the washer again by conveyor belt. All dust and slack collected here was compressed before transporting up to the pit tip. Some collieries transported this up to the tip by conveyor belt but Whitwell used dumper trucks. All new starters that had finished basic training wore yellow helmets, this was to easily identify you to everyone else as a new starter and that you were not accustomed to working in the mine. This was a good idea but the downside was that you were easily identified as a target for winding up and teasing. I was quite lucky whilst on the surface as I was never subject to that really.

I spent about a year on the surface due to the foreman telling me that I was a good worker and he needed extra help. I agreed to stay mainly because I enjoyed working on the surface all the teams there were great to work with. I was a little disappointed at not going underground straight away but I was under the impression that the job would be for life so there was plenty of time for that. The other disadvantage was the money was a lot less on the surface than underground. It was good to experience all aspects of the pit. The job I was aiming for was the banks man at number 1 shaft my Granddad was the first banks man at Whitwell and I thought it would be rather fitting to do that job. The foreman agreed to arrange a sneaky trip to the pit bottom at number 1 shaft one night on the night shift.

Fig 01
Whitwell number 1 shaft
Picture courtesy of nottsexminer

Pithead baths
Fig 5
Picture Courtesy of walespressphoto.com

CHAPTER 5

Working at Whitwell pit

It was about this time when I met Julia who was to become my 1ˢᵗ wife *(sounds bad I know)*. Julia lived in Hodthorpe with her parents her father was an ex conservative councillor which I knew would be an issue with my dad, my dad based friendships and acquaintances' by their politics rather than the person. Anyway that didn't deter me one bit, he did make it clear one day when I brought her to the house that she wasn't welcome, this was purely and simply based on her dads politics. I did point out that I wasn't going to choose my girlfriends or any other friends for that matter based on the political beliefs of either them or their family members. I know I thought it rather ridiculous but I knew my dad was a staunch believer in his extreme left wing views and the Whyles's were notorious for their stubbornness. We continued our relationship regardless but I didn't take her back to my home after that, I know dad would have been kind of ok with it but he would have been frosty.

Back at the pit I continued working on the surface or pit top as it was known continuing working on the screens, I preferred the night shift funnily enough, I suppose that was a little unusual for a young man in his prime but I liked it nonetheless. It was on one of these night shifts after twelve thirty when the coal production had stopped that the foreman asked me if I wanted to ride down to the pit bottom as he had promised.

I jumped at the chance knowing full well that there would have been hell to pay if we had got found out, anyway the winder and banks man were ok with it and the onsetter *(onsetter is another name for the banks man underground)* at the pit bottom was waiting to show me round. I entered the cage and was soon heading down the shaft at twelve miles per hour that sounds slow but in an enclosed shaft its bloody fast I can tell you. I arrived at the pit bottom and was shown briefly round, I was especially interested in the stables where the pit ponies were housed. I remember being amazed that they were still intact as if preserved for prosperity. That was an area of the pit that most miners never saw as man riding was mainly done at the number two shaft.

I told the onsetter that it was eerie down there and darker than most other places underground, he started to tell me that sometimes he can hear the ponies in the stables some distance behind his cabin. I said "ponies there are no ponies now, are there?" "No" he said, then the penny dropped, "you mean er... like ghost ponies", "yes" he said. I was intrigued and scared all at the same time, I then suggested I made my way back to the surface as I thought I would be missed. Fact of the matter is, I was uneasy now. That was my first visit underground at Whitwell pit. I enjoyed the experience and once back on the surface I was back in my comfort zone.

The pattern of the night shift was shift started at 10pm where the hand over from the afternoon shift was done, coal was produced constantly and the screens were running to keep up. At about 12:30am coal production eased off to a trickle and eventually stopped by 2am there was no production, we would be set on cleaning up from spillages and cleaning the Shecker, Sizer and belts not to mention the big electro magnet. At 2am it was snap time or break as you would probably know it as, 15 minutes for tea and sandwiches. 2:30am sharp the foreman would be kicking us out of the cabin to get us back to work cleaning. This would continue until 6am when the night shift ended and the day shift started, we would then head off to the pit baths for our shower before heading off home to bed. I would get home about 6:30am then go straight to bed and sleep until about 11: am then get up, the rest of the day was mine. I didn't sleep again until the end of the following shift. At that age sleep took up precious time. My dad would often go back to bed about 4pm before getting up at 7pm. To be fair my dad was obviously a lot older and his work was a hell of a lot harder than mine was. Most of my free time even then was spent round at Frankie Birds. Julia was at work at a knitwear factory in Worksop so when I was on nights we didn't see each other until the weekend.

Not all night shifts were the same however, sometimes there would be machine breakdowns on the screens which meant coal was stored in the mobile bunker then fed onto the screens once the breakdown had been fixed by the fitters, so this would mean that we would be coaling as we called it all night. Occasionally a collier would come to us at the screens asking if we had come across his adjustable spanner or other tool, we always said no but the truth is we had and we had claimed it. The Electro magnet was good at plucking spanners out of the coal.

One aspect of the night shift was the fitters coming to do the shaft exam. This is where they would stand on top of the cage and be lowered very slowly whilst they examined the shaft for damaged pipes and cables etc. They would blow a whistle every time they wanted the banks man to stop the cage. I found this quite intriguing. Slinging would also take place on the night shift after coaling had finished, this was where equipment would be chained under the cage or slung under the cage to be lowered into the pit. Sleeping was another activity or lack of it after coaling had finished, we would often find a hiding spot and drop off for a couple of hours once coaling and slinging had finished.

Working on the pit top was considered a cushy number and usually only people who could no longer work underground worked on the pit top, or people who had a medical condition that prevented them working in a dusty environment. I was working on there because I had been cohersed by the foreman. Ironically whenever I enquired about going underground I was always told that I was on the waiting list but I never really believed it. Some of the lads that I had trained with had been underground for months and were on a dam site more money than I was. Steve Cooling's dad was the banks man at number 1 shaft, I can remember watching him go to work as a boy and now I was working alongside him. Steve decided not to go to the pit, it would have been good to be working with him. Paul, Steve's older Brother was the banks man at number 2 shaft.

Another feature of the pit top was the tannoy system this was used to shout for fitters and electricians etc. that weren't in the fitting shop or electrical shop *(not shops as in buy, but cabins)*. The Tannoy was not a problem on the day shift but complaints were received at night time about the foul language that was heard in the village, the trouble is sound carries very far at night time. There was a very funny incident one night, our foreman Jim tried calling the fitters on the phone to fix a breakdown and got no response he then went to the tannoy and shouted *"fitters come in fitters, fitters needed on the screens, where the fuck are you hiding you idle bastards"*.

We reminded him about the ban on using the tannoy and bad language at night as it was 2:45am. He said "fuckin ell I forgot"

He pressed the button again and shouted "Sorry *I fuckin forgot I will try the fuckin phone again"*.

I can tell you we were in fits of laughter as he left to try the phone again.

Practical jokes were not uncommon either on nights, I remember one night we had just finished our cleaning and was heading off to the snap cabin, when one of the guys had got a latex mask in the guise of a very scary old man with scary white hair and eyes and mouth cut out, he said he was going to give the fitters a fright who were repairing a belt structure elsewhere on the screens, a couple of us decided to go to the belt structure where the fitters were working and started chatting to them, we had to climb a small ladder to get to where the fitters were. Some minutes after we heard a noise and turned towards the ladder where the noise had come from, when we saw this guy with just the head sticking up from the ladder with a cap lamp shining up from his chin, so all we could see was a glowing old wrinkly face. A couple of the fitters leapt off the structure scared out of their wits. It was very funny and before long complaints were made to management and these were banned. Thinking back now if you had a dodgy ticker it would have been easy to have a heart attack so it's easy to see why these masks were banned.

I remember one night cleaning the shecker when one of the lads thought it would be funny to start it up briefly whilst I was on it, it dam near shook my fillings out as I bounced down it onto the belt. I accept it might have been funny and I took it in good part, but I could quite easily have been seriously hurt had I got caught in one of the sizing plates. I never witnessed any serious accidents on the pit top but that was attributed more to luck than judgement.

Tom foolery or horse play was common place, especially on nights and it was a type of bonding. I never witnessed any bullying and I suspect it was a rare occurrence, Bullying is not acceptable in most walks of life and the coal mines were no exception. There were minor skirmishes however and they were sorted out quickly with nothing more than a bit of pushing and shoving. There were a few times when miners would wind each other up, for instance one night we were sat in our snap cabin on the pit top when one of the guys said to the guy sat next to me "have you got any nude pictures of your wife"? He said "No I fuckin haven't" He then said "do you want to borrow some?" Its wind ups like that where minor skirmishes start. But again I reiterate, it had no malicious intent.

The three shift system was ideal in a lot of ways because not all shifts suited everybody, I as I said earlier preferred the night shift. I detested the day shift with a passion, I just couldn't get to grips with getting up at 4:30am to walk to the pit and be changed and ready by 6:00am. The older guys however preferred the day shift and hated the night shift, taking advantage of that I swapped my day shifts for the night shift with other guys so that I was on nights regular. There was advantages and disadvantages with the shift pattern, for instance going off nights and returning on days meant that you would finish your night shifts on Saturday morning at 6:00am and be returning on Monday morning at 6:00. Conversely you could go off days at 2:00pm on Friday and be returning on Monday night at 10:00pm for the start of the night shifts. Swapping to nights regular meant your weekend was always the same length so really it was swings and roundabouts. It was just a matter of personal preference.

It was readily accepted that days was always the busiest shift, there was constant coal production and management were in abundance, afternoons shift less so, but nights was the most relaxed or at least on the pit top. And of course there was always a chance of getting your head down for a couple of hours.

One early morning after finishing a hard nights work (tongue planted in cheek) there was a note on my clock card to see the personnel officer, yep the obnoxious boss hog, As he worked 8 until 5 that meant I had to come back to the bloody pit during the day. I came back later that day, Frankie Bird kindly gave me a lift in. The personnel officer was in so I went into his office, the conversation went something as follows.

Knock knock knock

PO. "who is it?"

Me. "Steve Whyles, you wanted to see me"

PO. "Well what the fuck you standing there for bring thee sen in"
    I walked in and sat down in the chair.

PO. "Nar then young Ian, tha wants to goo darn pit"?

ME. "That's the general idea"

PO. "Clever little shit aren't tha"

ME. Silent

PO. "Suppose I was to let thee goo darn"

ME. "That would be great"

PO. "Tha waint think that when tha gets darn theer young un".

ME. "It's what I want to do and it's what I trained for".

PO. "So what will Jim think when I tell him tha dunt wanna work for him anymore"?

ME. "That's not the case I just wanna goo darn pit, Jim knows that"

PO. "as tha allast ad an ansa for everything, you little shit"

ME. Silent again

PO. "Anyway be at the time office Monday |Morning at 5:30am"

ME. "What for"?

PO. "A tha thick or sommat, tha gooin darn pit starting from Monday, so don't let me darn"

ME. "Yes!! Great thanks"

PO. "Tha will start 3 weeks CPS and will be mentored by a deputy, if tha fucks it up Al kick thee fuckin arse so fuckin ard that tha will be wiping thee arse through thi gob"

ME. "I waint let thee darn"

So, I was going down the pit at last, I was ecstatic. I could hardly wait to get back to the pit that night to tell all my workmates that I was going down the pit at last.

fig 001 view of Whitwell pit top
Picture courtesy of Phil Sangwell

CHAPTER 6

Going Underground

So I turned up for work that night, all my workmates knew already, it seems that Jim had told them. The first guy I came across was Bryan, he told me that Jim was not happy with me for going underground. I went into the cabin and Jim and the others were in there. I said good evening upon entering, the other guys responded but Jim just brushed passed me and left the cabin without speaking. I said *"What the fucks up with him"*? (*As if I didn't know*)

Pete said *"he's got the hump cos you're going downstairs, he's just been telling us that they won't give him anyone to replace you and he's well fucked off about it, I'd stay out of his way for a bit if I were you"*.

So I had to figure out how to play this one, Jim was a mardy bugger at the best of times. I decided to go to my work station while I decided what to do and how to approach him. Anyway I didn't have to worry as before long Pete came up onto my gantry and told me that Jim wanted to see me in the cabin and that he had been told to take over from me. So this was it, showdown. I headed off to the cabin a little bit apprehensive and found Jim sat waiting for me. I went in and shut the door and sat down.

Jim said *"wanna a cuppa?"*

I said "err, yeah, two sugars".

There was total silence while we waited for the water geyser to boil. Talk about a watched kettle, it seemed to take forever to boil. The geyser eventually boiled and Jim made the tea, he sat down and put my tea in front of me then said,

"*So you're going downstairs and leaving me in the shit, no fucking notice, no nothing*".

I told him that the timing wasn't mine, it was managements and that he had always known that I was on the waiting list, I also told him that they should have told him when they knew I was going. Jim then said

"*I know lad, I'm just fucked off that one of my best workers is going downstairs and they haven't anybody to replace you with. The lads were saying that they will miss you especially your knack of dropping one liners. I know we have locked horns a time or two but truth is I admire your readiness to stand your ground, you remind me of myself when I was your age*".

I was quite taken aback really, Jim had never intimated that he regarded me that highly before. I was almost sorry to be leaving. He finished by telling me that it was nigh on impossible to get out of the pit once down, and that it wasn't too late to change my mind. I couldn't help thinking, that even if I did change my mind there's no way on earth that I was going to tell boss hog that, he'd crucify me, literally. No, the decision is made, best stick to it. After all I have waited long enough.

The rest of the week passed off pretty well really, Jim was ok to a point but he did have his moments of mardiness as the week drew nearer to a close. There was no send off as such not even a good luck, from Jim but the guys did wish me well.

So the end of the week had come and gone and I was now making my way to the pit to start my underground CPS. The only downside at this stage was it was the day shift, here I have to be underground by 6:00am. So luckily Max the deputy was waiting for me and was soon taking me through the routine, off now to get my lamp and self-rescuer and my all-important check. The check system is where you are issued with two brass discs about the size of a two pence piece, one is round and the other is square. The checks or tally's as they were known by at Whitwell had your clock number on. This was different, my clock number was 2163, now it had changed to 609 and was stamped onto the discs. The tally system serves two purposes, when you arrive at the shaft side you hand the round one to the banksman he sends that by a vacuum system to the time office. This tells the time keeper that you have started your shift and are underground. If there was an emergency underground this tally would be used to identify who is underground, the square tally is handed to the banksman when you come back out of the pit. Likewise this is sent to the time keeper and that denotes the end of your shift, and more importantly should an emergency occur this will tell the rescue team that you are no longer underground. Your shift as I said ends when you have handed the square tally to the banksman so although you now head off to the pit baths for a shower you don't get paid for that. Some colliers did get paid for that in certain circumstances such as working in wet conditions, the deputy would give you what was known as a wet ticket and would enable you to shower in company time, this was known as bathing on the clock. It was not uncommon for this to be abused, sometimes some miners would ask the banksman to keep the tally back hence enabling the miner to bath on the clock, if miners came out of the pit early, which may or may not be for a valid reason the banksman would hold back the tally until the correct time. To be honest I think there is nothing wrong with that, after all it was only about ten minutes. On the other hand though the hours underground were seven and a quarter compared to eight hours on the surface.

So I went down for the first time at Whitwell, Max took me to the deployment board, this is where all miners assemble to be deployed to their assigned area of work, after my CPS period this is where I would report once down the pit. All miners were assigned areas by their tally number. I noticed mine and it said. 609 – with deputy on 2 foot. This meant that I was to accompany Max on the two foot seam. We proceeded off to the get on the paddy, this was a kind of open top train. The paddy ran from the pit bottom for a couple of miles. At the end if you were to go straight up you would be somewhere near Darfoulds near Worksop. (Interesting *note, the hump you can see at the toll bar at the bottom of Hodthorpe where the road intersects with the main A60 Mansfield – Worksop, is the hump caused by the main roadway that the paddy ran along.*) Max was always pointing out where we were in relation to the surface, I found this very interesting. We got off the paddy and then got on a man riding belt, this was a conveyor belt specifically for transporting miners, and we had been trained on this at Williamthorpe. Max took me through the process of getting on and off again. Simply put you had to jump on the belt on to your knees and lean forward otherwise you would be rolled over backwards. The important bit here was to keep your head down, standing up or sitting bolt upright would end in you getting a nasty clout to the head from the rings. You always had to face the direction of travel so as to prepare for getting off at the landing station, the belts did not stop, you got on and off whilst the belt was moving. The landing station was usually well lit and you could see it well before you arrived, to get off you had to crouch on your feet and step onto the landing platform walking forwards quickly, the phrase "hit the ground running has a significant meaning here". However should anybody miss the station there was an emergency stop bar across the belt that would stop the belt if anyone triggered it, also there was an emergency stop wire that ran the full length of the belt structure and could be easily activated if needed. So we got on the belt and rode it for a few minutes when Max turned round and said "get ready" I assumed the position, like an athlete in the starting blocks and stepped off a second after Max stepped off. It was easy, much easier than I thought it would be doing it for real. When we got off the landing station, we walked some distance and Max stopped and said "If you were to go straight up here you would come out at Van Dykes Nursery". I couldn't help but be intrigued, this area was known as 16â€™s and was a notorious area for rocks or boulders falling and also constantly wet. I suspected that many wet tickets were issued here.

We spent the rest of that shift patrolling the areas and checking on the work areas. The only exciting bit during the shift was the shot firing in the main header, the shots had been prepared but mostly the deputy fired them. I remember being told to take cover in the manhole round the corner as Max fired the shot, a slight pause then a thud, ears popped then a cloud of dust. That was the first time I had ever witnessed an explosive detonation close up.

After that we patrolled further, inspecting equipment and machines for signs of fire. Sounds daft but slack and dust builds up near moving parts such as on rollers on conveyor belts, this causes friction and that is a big danger of fire breaking out. The sobering thought was that if a major fire broke out on the intake side then apart from the risk of explosion, smoke would billow through the rest of the mine, carried by the air. The self-rescuers would only give an oxygen supply for a maximum of ninety minutes. Imagine trying to make your way to the pit bottom in a smoke filled tunnel in pitch darkness and with the chemicals from the self-rescuer burning your throat, and the smoke burning your eyes, It would be absolute chaos. Then if you made it the cage could only wind twenty four men at a time, and there could be easily two to three hundred men to evacuate. It could quite easy take well over an hour to get everyone out, remember you only have ninety minutes of air and that means if you were working two miles away from the pit bottom, you would have to make it in thirty minutes in the conditions described above. Sobering is it not?

The risks of being killed underground were numerous, the training we did hammered that point home very heavily. I need not emphasise all the dangers, suffice to say they are just as apparent as in most industries with the exception of being in a confined space underground.

After a couple of days with Max he decided that I was ready in his view to be placed with a team. So I spent the next few weeks going with different teams, this is where you harden up, colliers were notorious for being tough, they had to be (colliers is the common name for face and heading workers). I took lots of teasing and piss taking, harmless really but intimidating nonetheless. The yellow helmet made you a target. I had comments about my sex life, my dad, and my mother, who was sleeping with my girlfriend whilst I was down the pit. Nothing was out of bounds, and I do mean nothing.

The next couple of weeks carried on with going down the pit, going to the deployment board to see which team I would be working with, that was as I said being on the market. Most of the work was being on a button, stopping and starting machines all in very noisy environments.

One day I was at the deployment board when I noticed that I had been assigned to a team of my own with two other lads, just so happened I had trained with these lads. We were to be our own haulage team. Haulage was where supplies and materials were transported to the face in tubs, tubs were on bogies which travelled on rails that ran throughout the pit. The rails had a wire rope that ran the length which was controlled by a winding engine on one end, there was a driver who controlled the winder and the rest if the team used to signal instructions via the wires that ran overhead, this was 2 wires and we had to cross the wires with a spanner to make the circuit and ring at the engine, there was a set code. Haulage was considered one of the most dangerous activities underground and was the cause of many an accident. However we were told to report to the pit bottom and to take it in turns being the team leader. We had practised fastening the tubs onto the rope using pig tail clips, then tightened with a spanner. There were set rules as to how many tubs you could take, depending on the weight of the load, four was the norm but if transporting big heavy roof masters then two was the absolute limit.

We carried on doing this for quite a few weeks, when one morning shift we were clipping two roof masters to the rope to take to the face, we were just about to head off with the load knowing that the trip to the face and the return with empties would take all shift. When a deputy came up to us and said "where a tha gooin wi them"?

(Me) "Where gooin to 2 foot".
(Deputy) "Why as tha only got 2"?
(Me) "Cos that's all we can tek, they're masters".
(Deputy) "A can see what thee are ya clever twat, why ant tha tekkin fooer? The fuckin face will stop cos tha too fuckin scared to tek more than two, nar clip two more on an get a move on".
(Me) "We can't tek fuckin fooer, we'll get fuckin shot".
(Deputy) "Tha'll get more than that if I av to tell the ageean, na fuckin shift it". So we clipped two more on and headed off, as it was a long way we rode on the back clip, this was highly dangerous and the cause of many a nasty accident, and it was a sackable offence. We were supposed to walk alongside them. We arrived at a manhole (cut out in the side wall, purpose was for stepping out of the way of large loads and runaway tubs) the manhole had a large transformer in, and as this would be warm we decided to stop there and wait until all the colliers had passed as they would be walking. We have held colliers up before by blocking the way and paid the price for it. As we were also on the brow of a steepish hill, we decided to retighten the clips, this is done by signalling the load just over the brow of the hill, and removing the front clip, the only way to do this was by standing in between the rails and unscrewing the clamping bolt with the spanner. This is highly dangerous because if the back clip let go then you were a gonna, remember we had

four masters weighing nearly four tons, twice the allowed load. So one of the other two members of my team rang the signal to take the load over the brow and I unfastened the front clip, the signal was rung again to jolt all the weight on the rear clip. I then stood back in the rails to replace the front clip on tight. This went to plan, so we went into the manhole whilst he colliers had passed.

The colliers came by dropping their usual sarcastic remarks, and of course we returned the compliments. The colliers had been gone down the hill about five minutes if that when we heard a large rumble, we jumped off the transformer and ran out to where the masters were waiting, and to our horror, they weren't there, they were heading off down the hill on their own. The rear clip had slipped and the weight just pulled them down the hill. My initial fear was that the men had not long since gone and they would have been wiped out by the masters, at least thirty men were down there. When the dust settled we ran down to find that the masters had derailed and wiped out electrical cables and the conveyor belt structure and had become entangled in the belt. Luckily the men had just gone round the corner and were at least a hundred yards ahead of the melee.

Bloody hell were we in for the high jump now, fresh out of training and breaking the rules, rules which were there for a reason, to prevent what had just happened from happening. I feared we would be sacked for gross negligence.

It just so happened by sheer luck that the deputy who made us take four masters came and said, "There were four masters in two lots of two, not four on one load, as tha got that whyles'y"? (Me) "Yeah ok but will we still be in for it"? (Deputy) "Tha will av to explain this sen to gaffa, but my report will say thar add two lots of two, if tha SES any different al fuckin kill thi, as tha got that"? (Me) "Got it". We headed out of the pit with the deputy to see the pit manager, I was shitting myself as was the other two, but more so me because I was the team leader that day.

The Manager said "who's *the team leader*"?

(Me)   "I *am gaffer*"
(Manager) "Then start by telling me what the fuck has happened, and why you have closed down half of my fuckin pit".

I explained the sequence of events just as the deputy had told us to. The Manager asked the other two if they had anything to add and did they agree with my statement, they agreed and didn't add anything. The Manager asked us to wait outside while he spoke to the deputy. We waited outside his office like naughty schoolboys. The deputy came out five minutes later and said "right lads lets av ya back darn pit". I asked him what was going to happen, he told us that the incident was over, we hadn't done anything wrong, but he was to keep his eye on us for a while. Then he looked at us and winked, a wink that said we got away with that one.

CHAPTER 7

The run up to the 1984-5 Strike

So it is the start of 1984, a year that would change my life forever, not that I had any idea at this stage. The year started much the same as any other. I remember one particular shift on the afternoon shift, my team and I were setting off taking a load of rings (girders) to the coal face. We set off as usual, riding the clip, as usual, except it was far from usual it was a pig of a load and overloaded as usual. We got about half an hour in when the rope haulage stopped, we hadn't signalled for it to stop, I went to find a phone to phone the haulage rope driver who was some way away from where we were. The driver answered his phone.

(Me)	"What's *up wi rope?*"
(Driver)	"Fucked *if I know, it just fuckin stopped*"
(Me)	"As *tha tried resetting it*"?
(Driver)	"Of course a fuckin av, dus tha think am an idiot or summat"?
(Me)	"As tha rung sparkies"? (*Sparkies are what we called electricians*)
(Driver)	"no a dunt know what the fucks up wi it, I thought it woh stuck or summat".
(Me)	"Foh fuck sake al fuckin ring um mi sen". I put phone down to start another call to sparkies when I heard a

---

yell. I turned round and saw one of my team on the floor underneath one of the trams.

(Me)　　　　　"Kinell a tha allrate marra"?

(Team mate)　"Yeah a thought add just av a lie down foh a minute, of course am not allrate the fuckin thing is on mi leg".

I immediately bashed the clip handle with my adjustable spanner to release the clip from the rope that would stop the load moving again if the rope surged again. Me and the remaining team mate tried to lift up one side of the tram but obviously it was too heavy for just two of us, just then the disctrict deputy came running up with two other guys, they snapped the bindings holding the rings on and started to off load the rings. Before long the load was off and we managed to pull him out, he had a very bad burn from the steel rope on the right side of his waist. The deputy then took him off to get medical attention with the other guys and told us to get the load to the face sharpish. I got back onto the phone and rang the haulage rope driver.

(Me)　　　"What the fuck appened theer tha ran mih mate ower ya fuckin idiot" he said" it want me it wah stuck and it just released by its sen"

(Me)　　　"Well dint tha ave fuckin brake on"?

He said "what's the point of avin brake on tha daft cunt, it's not fuckin workin"?

(Me)　　　"it ant dun a bad job of crushin a man to say it's not fuckin workin, ave sparkies bin yet"?

(Driver)　"No a shunt need em now as fukin leets on nar to say its all rate"

(Me)　　　"rate am gunna give a start and stop signal and see if its wockin before I clip back up". I rang the signal to start, after a few seconds the rope started moving again, so I rang the stop signal and the rope sure enough stopped. I asked the other team mate how our guy got trapped under the tram, he said that he was jumping on the tensioned rope to see if he could set it free, and it shot backwards knocking him off his balance and then shot forwards over him whilst he was laid on the roadway. I said that he was fucking lucky he didn't get killed.

We reloaded the rings and binded them up the best we could, then we clipped up and set off. This time we didn't ride the rope just in case.

We got to the heading and one of the colliers came over.

(Collier) "where the fucks tha bin wih them, wiv bin waitin ere foh fuckin ever, a bet thas bin tossin it off some weer".

(Me) "There's bin an accident and one of arr guys got hurt"

(Collier) "woh he ridin fuckin rope"?

(Me) "No e fuckin want, but thanks foh thi concern"

(Collier) "ave less on thi lip or thill be another fucker bein carried owt pit, an it waint be no fuckin accident nah get them fuckin rings off loaded ya lill clever twat, wait while A see thi faather".

So we started off loading sharpish, I wasn't the brightest spark in the box but I was clever enough to know you don't mess with colliers.

We were stacking the rings at the roadside with one of us on each end, I was walking backwards and my team mate was walking forwards when he tripped pushing the ring into me and causing me to fall backwards and letting go of the ring, it dropped straight onto my leg, Jesus that bugger hurt, I was sure that my leg was broken. The colliers came running over and lifted the ring off my leg,

(Collier) "Ah tha allrate mi old cock, can tha move thi leg"

(Me) "Yes"

(Collier) "Then why dint tha fuckin move it art on way ya daft bugger"? "sit thi sen there an al get fost aider to sort thee art". He gets on phone which was just above my head, and I heard him say

"Urry thi sen up laurel and fuckin ardy are in need of thi elp".

Despite all the bravado they were concerned and got me some assistance, it turned out that my leg was badly bruised and nothing more, but I was very lucky.

———

After being looked over by the first aider, I could barely walk due to the bruising, the deputy for the district was concerned that I was miles away from a man riding belt and I wouldn't have been able to get on and off safely if it was closer. We decided the best way was to ride on the empty trams or call for a stretcher, I opted to ride the tram. The deputy got us clearance to ride the tram to the paddy station which was only twenty minutes away. On arrival to the pit top it was straight to the medical room to be looked at closely. After being examined it was off home to rest for a couple of days. The medical examiner told me that I was the third leg injury that day. The sobering thing is anyone of those accidents could just have been fatal had the circumstances been different. Mining machinery does not stop at blood, they tend to be very hard and unforgiving. I had learned my lesson about riding the clip as tempting though it was. Colliers and mine workers look out for each other, they had to do because we all depended on each other to watch our backs. Colliers and mine workers tended to be tough but much disciplined.

Another incident I witnessed was thoroughly unbelievable, I was deployed on one night shift on a button on 16's main gate (near Van Dyke's), when the deputy came to say he wanted me in another district as a haulage team were a man down after yet another accident. On our way down the deputy stopped by a manhole (wall cut-out) there was a number of donkey jackets hung up in there, in one of the pockets was a large plastic pop bottle full of what looked like orange squash. The deputy took the bottle out of the pocket and showed me the black line that had been painted on so that the owner would know if anyone had drunk out of it. He drank a good swallow and the mark was about two inches away from the pop level now, the deputy took the bottle over behind a machine then returned showing me that the pop was now back where it should be. I asked him how he had filled it and he gave me the bottle and told me to put it back in the pocket. I took the bottle from him and it was warm, I mean very warm, I turned to the deputy and he winked at me before I could ask the obvious question that told me the answer. Whilst continuing down to the haulage team waiting for me the deputy, said

"back there young un, if anyone asks thee owt, remember tha saw fuck all, that guy who owns that bottle is messing about wi my missus, they both think I dunt know, so I piss in his pop every fuckin day".

I can remember seeing the hurt and anger in his eyes, and I did feel sorry for him then he said "I used to think it wa the thermal blankets keeping my side of the bed waarm, till I fun art about that cunt".

I smirked, then

He said "yeah fuckin funny, let's hope no fucker shags your missus while tha darn ere, cos then tha will know what fuckin real pain is young un".

We continued in silence for the rest of the way. When we got there, the deputy said

"nah then young un, I know tha likes to know we're thar are, so if you were to go straight up from here thad get fuckin wet cos we're under Welbeck lakes".

He was right I did find all that stuff fascinating. I joined the team and we continued the shift transporting supplies to the face.

In February there was a spate of locker thefts in the baths, apparently some toe rag had been stealing wages out of the lockers in the pit head baths, When on the night shift we used to collect our wages from the time office when getting to the pit before the start of shift, which meant that you had little choice but to put them in the locker overnight. So whoever was stealing was one of us. The baths had an attendant but people were walking in and out of the baths at all times. I'm not sure the culprit ever got caught but there were no murders so presumably not. One had to be pretty low to steal a man's wages and I am absolutely certain that he would have been lynched had he been caught and rightly so.

Towards the end of February the talk underground was all about the government wanting to close some pits, this fired up the men beyond belief, eventually there was talk of strike action. I remember that one night turning up on nights we had to assemble in the canteen, we were told by the union that the Tories wanted to decimate our livelihood and close twenty pits, he wanted a show of hands from us for strike action, there was at least 150 men in there and when he asked for all those in favour, a lot of hands went up, then he said "all those against". Then the rest of the hands went up including mine. It was overwhelmingly evident that the vote was against strike action. The union upon giving the results to the area NUM said that Whitwell had voted to strike. That infuriated me, I know there was two other shifts and a total of eight hundred and fifty men, and they could, I emphasise could have voted in favour. A few days later I saw the union guy in the yard, I approached him and said

"What were the results of the days and afters shift? You told the area that we had voted to strike so what was the count?"

He never stopped walking but turned and said

"Whitwell voted to strike, that's all you need to know".

I spoke with other miners whilst on shift and other shifts after that, it was clear that the result was close but I felt that we had been duped by the Union, my thought was the men voted not to strike which was going against the unions recommendations, and as the vote was just a show of hands there would be no way of knowing what the true feeling of the men was. I was beginning to lose faith in the union by now, my political beliefs were neither one way nor the other, I believed that no matter what colour the flag they all shit in the same pot.

I spoke to my dad about it when getting home and it was overwhelmingly clear that he was a thousand percent in favour of the strike. I told him that I wasn't sure it would be a good thing and that I didn't want to strike. He told me that Thatcher was trying to close down the coal mines and we had to show solidarity with the Yorkshire lads cos there coming out. Once theres a picket line at Whitwell nobody will be working we will all be out until we have brought this tory government down. I said I wasn't sure I would strike until we had a national ballot, I remember his words to this very day, and they were,

"If you're gonna live under my roof you'll be out on strike wi rest on us, tha dunt cross picket lines"

I asked him when we were going to get a national ballot, he told me we didn't need one.

I went to my girlfriend's house as usual for a couple of hours before work, we had been looking at houses in the village for weeks and had made an offer for one on Welbeck Street. Her dad said that he had heard on the news that there was talk of strike action. I told him that I didn't think that a strike would change anything and that we would lose out, I didn't believe that there were really any winners of strike action. I then told him about the conversation I had with my dad. He told me that he knew how I must be feeling and that he thought the same as I did, he then went on to say that if that was the case then I would be very welcome to move in with them, he told me that me and his daughter were committed to each other but that aside you can come here if it helps but it's your decision I will support you however you decide. This helped me at last someone was actually reinforcing that I am an individual and an adult and most importantly that I didn't have to be dictated to by being told what I have to believe.

This I don't mind telling you was a difficult time for me, I had always had the utmost respect for my dad, he was my dad and I loved him absolutely no question of that, but on the other hand I know he loves me but he's made it clear that I wasn't welcome in that household if I didn't follow his and the union's diktat. So I am now realising that blood is actually not thicker than water and that he was prepared to disown me over a political belief. This was a shock to me and I had an awful lot of thinking to do. I talked it over with my older Brother as he was married and had a family of his own, his advice was to do what I thought was right he wouldn't judge me either way. He wasn't connected with the coal mines other than having a brother and father working there. His advice was helpful and above all I knew that if the worst came to the worst and I actually did cross a picket line then at least he wouldn't disown me too. All this and there was no strike as yet other than sporadic pickets here and there.

Soon after on March the 5th, the leader of the NUM Arthur Scargill announced to the world on TV that the NUM had instructed all its members to come out on strike and that the strike was now in force. Jesus, now I had a problem and a bloody big one at that, things had moved very quickly.

I was still living at home and I could now not go to work. I spoke to my girlfriend about it, and she said that we needed to speak to her dad again. So we went back to her house and her dad was sitting in the front room watching the news, which just so happened to be full of the strike. I asked him if he had got a minute. He said

"Yes son sit down".

I sat down in the armchair facing him and said,

"You obviously know what's going on" he said

"yes the news is full of nothing else, I know you're having a tough time of it at the moment, but what I said the other day still stands, you are welcome in my house and you are free to decide what you want to do, there is no pressure from me, I believe the strike would be wrong but you're working there and only you can decide. But I will help in any way I can, just ask".

He told me that I was entitled to make a choice and that was my right, if I stayed at home that choice would be taken away from me.

I was on nights but had heard that the afternoon shift had gone out on strike and were picketing the pit. I turned up for work on the nights and was met by a few pickets, they said

"Tha can't goo in theer lad's weer art".

I was with a couple of my mates. I turned to the union guy and said

"Since fuckin when, I aint had no ballot except for that joke of one the other neet, until a national ballot says otherwise I'm gunna work"

The union guy then said

"Tha dunt cross picket lines"

I knew some men were already inside the pit but not many and none were underground yet. I turned to my mate and asked him if he was working or striking, he said he was working. I turned back to the union guy and said

"Sorry weer gooin in we aint voted to strike and until a national ballot ses otherwise we aint coming art.

It turned out that not enough men had crossed the picket line to operate the mine safely, so we stood about on the pit top all night chatting. Most of the men made it clear that they wouldn't cross the picket tomorrow, After all it will be over in a week or two.

So then that was it we were out on strike! like it or lump it. We had given in to an undemocratic union who had no mandate for a strike and at a time when coal stocks were at an eleven year high and at the start of spring. This is a non-starter surely, what was Scargill thinking of?

So I didn't go to work the following shift, at home my dad was kicking off about my going in to work previously. That was it I was going to take the girlfriend's dad up on his offer. So I packed my bags and moved out. I and the girlfriend were half way through buying our first house anyway and our offer had been accepted so we were committed now. I was under added pressure of being committed to a mortgage and being unable to meet the payments. Fantastic! Bloody fantastic! On the brighter side there was a slight hold up and the contracts wouldn't be exchanged for some weeks yet. Further to that our wedding had been booked for November 1984 long before the strike came along.

CHAPTER 8

During the Strike

So I was now living with my fiancée and her parents, already feeling abandoned and disowned by my parents. My Fiancée's parents were absolutely amazing and supportive to me and with no pressure whatsoever.

I agonised over what to do about the situation for Months, I knew I had a monumental decision to make. I had to consider what would happen by going back to work, I had seen the images on the news on TV and knew that violence and intimidation would be a real possibility not only to me but to my Fiancée and her parents, fire bomb attacks on houses in Nottinghamshire were taking place, it was fast turning into a civil war quite literally. Then I had to consider what would happen by staying out on strike. Could I put aside my gut feelings and concede to the masses, sure! That would be the easiest option, but then I was allowing Arthur Scargill to dictate what I was to do with my life. My personal belief then and more so now is that Arthur Scargill was using the miner's for his own political ambitions, I had watched many a TV interview with him and his stance and rhetoric were always the same. I know he was a great orator but then dictators usually are. I had heard that he was going to be coming to Whitwell miners' welfare to give one of his by now well-rehearsed speeches. I decided I was going to go to that meeting, you never know he might just announce a national ballot.

I went along to the meeting and my dad was on the door, as I walked in he stuck a "Coal not dole" sticker on my jacket front, I immediately pulled this off and threw it to the floor, The BBC were filming this meeting as part of their Panorama programme. Scargill did his usual thing and made his speech at the top of his voice, I was sat on the floor as the hall was packed out, I was disgusted with what I heard, and it was blatantly obvious now that a national ballot was not going to be forthcoming. I made my mind up then that I had to return to work, if I was not going to be allowed my democratic right to a vote then I was going to vote with my feet.

When I got back to my Fiancée's house I told my Fiancée that I needed to discuss going back to work with her. She told me she was ok with it, She was fully behind me, She worked at a clothing factory in Worksop and so did a lot of miners wives. I pointed this out to her but her resolve was as strong as mine. I told her that I would sit on it for a few days while I weighed up the pros and cons then I would speak to her mum and dad.

The Panorama programme aired on the following Monday night, we all watched it and from the comments my fiancées father was making it was clear that I had his full support. After the programme had finished, I took a sideways glance at my Fiancée and raised my eyebrows, she understood immediately and nodded. This was it I was going to tell him, I asked her father if I could have a word, he said "certainly - let's go in the other room away from the TV".

I said "As you know, I have been agonising over the decision to go back to work for quite some time now"

(Her father) "Yes I know lad"

(Me) "Well I have been hanging on in the vain attempt of getting a national ballot, there was no mention of getting this at the meeting and as we have just seen every time the question is asked he deliberately turns the question round, just like a politician that he aspires to be".

(Her father) "Hmm yes, clearly the guy is obsessed with trying to bring down the government"

(Me) "Well I have made my mind up that I should go back to work, it is the right thing to do, some of my mates are already back and that makes about eleven men so far"

(Her father) "Steve I told you from the start of all this that the decision is yours and yours alone, We told you that we would support you in whatever you decided, it's a decision that quite frankly I don't envy you, it must have been awful for you, however, it's clear you have toiled with this for some months, I don't want you feeling you are obliged to us for supporting you financially during the past few months, you are as far as we are concerned part of this family and to help you in your time of need is not only our duty but also our pleasure"

(Me) "I know that you have been behind me and that has made the decision easier, it's just that things will get very hairy from now on for all of us not just me".

(Her father) "Then so be it! Like you said the other day mob rule should never overcome, it's not democracy, it's not right. I'm proud of you, whatever happens from here on in will serve to strengthen our resolve"

I don't mind admitting that I was close to tears, a big weight was lifted off my shoulders and I had a man here that had put his faith in me 100% no question, a few months ago he didn't even know me and here he is telling me how proud he is and even willing to risk damage to his car and house because of me, this man was a true saint in my eyes.

So this is it the time has come, I will telephone the colliery manager tomorrow morning, to see how to proceed.

True to my word I picked up the telephone and I was shaking, this was harder than I thought it would be, there would be no going back once I had made this call. I rang the number, then the answer came.

(Switchboard) "Good Morning Whitwell Colliery how can I help"?
(Me) "Can I speak to the Manager please"?
(Switchboard) "Yes - who is calling please"?
(Me) "Steve Whyles"
(Switchboard) "One moment please"

The phone rang for what seemed like ages, then, the call was answered again.

(Manager) "Hello Mr Whyles, do you require a secure line"?

(Me) "Err yes I suppose"

(Manager) "Ok, I have the number you are calling from, I will ring you straight back"

(Me) "Ok"

I replaced the handset and waited for the phone to ring. A few moments later the phone sure enough rang. I answered.

(Me) "Hello"

(Manager) "Hello, is that Stephen"?

(Me) "Yes gaffer"

(Manager) "Now then Stephen, how can I help you"?

(Me) "I have been against the strike from the start and I've been out on strike only whilst awaiting a national ballot"?

(Manager) "I know, Stephen, we had an idea that you and some others were against the strike"

(Me) "Really, well I have made my mind up that I want to come back, I always have, but you know how it is"

(Manager) "yes, only too well," if you want me too, I can make arrangements then ring you back this afternoon, is that ok"?

(Me) "Yes gaffer"

Well! That's it, I have made a move. I felt kinda strange in a way, I knew it was the right thing to do, that I was certain of, but what will happen now is anybody's guess.

My Fiancées father came through and asked me if I was alright, I told him I was. He told me that I had done the right thing and not to worry about the consequences we would deal with them as they arose.

Later that afternoon the phone rang, I answered it as I was expecting the all-important call.

(Me) "Hello"

(Caller) "Hello its Mr Vardy, can I speak to Stephen Whyles please"?

(Me)   "Hello gaffer, speaking"

(Manager) "The arrangements have been made son, the bus will pick you up Monday morning at your girlfriends address"

(Me)   "Why Monday? Why not tomorrow? And how did you know I was at my girlfriends"?

(Manager) "Ok, the arrangements have to be coordinated with the police, so they can arrange police cover at your address, this usually takes a couple of days and that takes us to the weekend. I was informed by a colleague that you had moved out as your dad had mentioned it to someone and he passed that information on. We keep tabs on all people on our list that we think are the most likely to return, we have to do that, also we need to make sure that there is no one planted in here by the union, that has been known to have happened at other pits"

(Me)   "I see, so what happens now"?

(Manager) "you will receive a call from the police and they will explain the procedure for being picked up, don't worry you're in safe hands, I will give you a number to ring which is a direct line to the fast response police, you may not need it but, we have to be realistic"

(Me)   "I can just walk down the railway line gaffer that runs straight outside our house into the pit yard"

(Manager) "No you can't son that is not safe, you need to be under police protection at all times"

He then gave me the number, and I wrote it down on the pad.

(Manager) "Stephen, you have done the right thing, you're not alone. You have friends here who will help you, I'm not going to tell you it will be easy, you're not stupid, I suspect you've seen the news, but we will be with you and supporting you, you're in safe hands, take care lad and I will see you on Monday"

(Me)   "Ok gaffer, see you Monday"

So that was it, I did feel better in a way, that was the longest conversation that I have ever had with him since we trashed half the pit with the roof masters.

My Fiancées father came through and said, "Everything ok? Is there anything I can help with"?

(Me)   "Well, I've done it, the police will call sometime before Monday to give me the arrangements, I feel better but scared all at the same time,"

(Fiancées father) "Well done lad, I'm proud of you, I know how difficult that was for you, don't worry were behind you"

Within an hour or two there was a knock on the door, I was in the hallway so I answered it, I was stunned to see two policemen.

(Police)   "Could I speak to Stephen Whyles Please?"
(Me)   "That's me"
(Police)   "don't look so scared lad, can we come in"?
(Me)   "Err yes of course cone in"

I showed them through to the sitting room, my fiancées father cane through and asked if we wanted a cuppa, we all said yes.

He left to make the cuppa and shut the door behind him.

(Police)   "now then Stephen, we have come to tell you what will happen on Monday morning, and to answer any questions you might have"
(Me)   "Yes ok"
(Police)   "the bus will pick you up at your garden gate at five fifteen monday morning, before that there will be police in and around your garden area, so don't get alarmed, I need to know what enemies you may have and who you would most expect trouble from"

(Me)   "Well, I don't have what I would class as enemies, but from Monday morning I'm gonna have eight fuckin hundred"

(Police) "laugh" "that's the spirit, no harm will come to you, and we'll make sure of that".

(Me)   "Do you expect there to be any"

(Police) "Not really, there are a few hotheads but we know who they are, you have our fast response number do you"?

(Me)   "Yes"

(Police) "Then if you get any problems ring that number we will be here in minutes"

(I)   "ok, thank you"

(Police) "The police will be mets, not the local police but don't let that worry you, they are well used to civil unrest and they are the guys to have around, make no mistake about that"

They left before the tea arrived, so I sat with the family and told them the plans, I was worried about the mets, though, we had seen them on the news, and they were stationed in Grantham in Lincolnshire and were notoriously tough.

So it was Thursday and I would have until Monday to fester about what I had just done.

That night I didn't sleep too well, all sorts of things were running through my head.

The following morning I got up about eight, my girlfriends father was in the kitchen masking tea, he asked me if I wanted a cuppa, then told me that my dad was at the garden gate at five this morning, just hanging around and staring at the house. I wondered why that was, then the penny had dropped.

(Me)   "God!! He must know, but how? I haven't told a soul, nobody"

(Fiancées father) "neither have we, but my brother rang me earlier to say he had seen him as he was in his way to work, you're right he must know, there can be no other reason he would be there at that time"

(Me)	"Right!! I'm going up to see him and find out, who does he think he is"?
(Fiancées father)	"I know you must be angry, but don't do anything rash"
(Me)	"No I won't but this has to be sorted"

I had my tea then set off walking the half mile or so to his house.

I was shaking with rage, I got there and knocked on the door and just walked in, my Mother was at the kitchen sink.

| (Me) | "Where is he"? |
| (My mother) | "in other room" |

I walked straight through to the front room, he was standing in the corner sorting out some scratch cards he was selling in aid of the Militant tendency.

(Me)	"What were you doing outside my fiancée's house at five this morning?
(Dad)	"I went to try to talk some sense into you"
(Me)	"Sense!! What about"
(Dad)	"I have been told that you're going back to work, you're going to Scab!"
(Me)	"You know what my feelings are about this bloody strike, we not gonna get a ballot and I'm not gonna be dictated to by fuckin commy Scargill! or you for that matter"
(Dad)	"you don't cross picket lines, when this is all over and done with you still have to live with what you have done and live in the village you will be branded a scab and once a scab always a scab no son of mine is going to scab"
(Me)	"Ok if that's the way you want it, fine!"

I stormed out slamming the door on my way, I was angry, hurt, and upset, and my own father would disown me for exorcising my right to work. I couldn't believe it. I was well aware of the impact it would have on him, After all he was a prominent figure both in the community and on the picket line, I could see that it would be embarrassing, but hang on, he couldn't care less what I was going through, he never looked me in the eyes, he carried on fumbling with the bloody scratch cards as if he was just thinking out loud.

I got back to my fiancees house, they could see I was visibly upset and angry. They were quick to calm me down somewhat, but that hurt and yes betrayal and abandonment was very hard and painful to accept even today some thirty years on.

CHAPTER 9

Crossing the Picket line

Sunday night, I decided to go to bed early due to having to get up at four o'clock. The night was a very restless one, I tossed and turned all night long. I kept getting up for a drink and then the toilet, and a little bit of pacing up and down like an expectant father. I don't think I slept more than thirty minutes at a time that night. I was in my own room as my fiancees father was a traditionalist and wouldn't entertain us sleeping together before marriage. That was good tonight I didn't want to disturb my fiancée, as she was at work too in the morning. In reality though I don't think anybody slept much that night, such was the enormity of what was going to happen in the morning.

I got up just before 4am and looked through the curtains, all was quiet nit a soul about. I went into the bathroom and had a wash then went downstairs, my fiancées mum and dad were already up, her mum was cooking breakfast, The mere thought of eating just made me feel sick, I can't eat as soon as I get up at the best of times, but my stomach was in knots, there was no way I was going to eat bacon eggs and beans and keep it down, not today anyway.

Very little was said apart from reassuring words of encouragement and approval. My fiancée was up and she was worried too but tried not to show it.

At Ten past five there was a knock in the door, my fiancées father answered it and it was a policeman, he came back into the kitchen and told me the bus was 3 minutes away and to be ready. Jesus now my heart was pounding, I thought it was gonna beat right out of my chest. I got my snap that had been packed for me, I had not even given that a thought, but they had. I headed for the door and opened it, my god, police everywhere, now I'm well and truly shitting mi sen, the bus came over the bridge and pulled up at the gate. It was an old east midland green single Decker it had weld mesh all the way round it covering all the windows. I walked up the path between the police officers and one of the policemen opened the gate, the door of the bus opened. There I could see the driver and his mate at the front of the bus with crash helmets on, my arse cheeks were well and truly twitching now. I headed to the door and stepped on.

(Driver's mate) "come *on lad well done, you're among friends now*"

Then I heard calls from down the bus practically in unison one after the other.

(Miners)   "come *on Stevie lad well done mate we're proud on thee, come and sit thi sen darn*"

I looked down the bus and saw at least eight men, all of which I knew. I sat down on the right side of the bus and the bus set off towards the pit, the lads started chatting and some cone over to sit near me. I remember Gordon Butler of the NUM saying that all the working miners were issued with Mickey Mouse masks in the busses. This certainly wasn't true in this case, no attempt was made by any of them to hide their identity.

(Miner)   "dunt *worry this is the worst bit to come but it gets easier I'm telling thee, dunt let it put the off*"

I was starting to feel better now and chatting to my work mates made it an easier pill to swallow. Until we approached the pit bridge that is.

We came to the pit bridge and as we started going up onto the brow, the driver's mate shouted "here we go lads"

As we went over the bridge, I could see literally hundreds and hundreds of picketers lining both sides of the road, they erupted into spontaneous chants and shouting, it was absolutely bedlam, now my heart was racing faster than it had ever gone before, I was petrified to a degree, the other lads on the bus were quite amused at the pickets, some of the words I picked out from the melee was *"Judas!" "Scabs!" "Bastard's"*. We got the lot hurled at us, this continued all the way down into the pit yard which was some quarter of a mile distance, the pickets were pushing trying to break the police lines that were linked arm in arm to hold them back. There was camera flashes galore. We drove into the pit and then it started to quieten down a bit. That was 5 minutes if terror I don't mind telling you. That was by far the hardest and most frightening thing I have ever done in my life bar nothing!

When the bus stopped one of the lads said. "Well *what did tha reckon to that?"*

(Me)	"Jesus *fuckin Christ that was something else, I thought it would be bad but fuckin ell, am sheckin like a shitting dog"*
(Miners)	"yeah *I know, it dunt get any woss than that mate, and it does get easier, thas done the hard bit and let me tell thi sommat else, a lot of them art theer want to do what we're doin, but they aint got the fucking balls, shit scared they are, fuckin hypocrites"*.
(Me)	"Shit *scared, Jesus that just about sums me up when we came ower that fuckin bridge"*
(Miners)	"Ah *know and if tha sed tha want scared, tha wood ave bin lying"*
(Me)	"I *feel allrate nah tho, but I can't believe av actually done what av been wanting to do for months"*
(Miners)	"Well *done lad, thas got some balls, al gi thi that, nah lets goo and get a brew"*

The best way to describe that experience is that it's a bit like watching the news when some murderer or child killer is going into court in the back of the police van, and all the onlookers are trying to get to the van. It felt just like that must feel to them, except we were not murderer's we were not child killers, we were just ordinary working class men going into work.

I was being forced into enduring all this because Arthur Scargill wants to bring down the Tory government using the miners. The miners were just too blind to see it.

We went inside and met the others that had gone in. I was welcomed by them and we exchanged experiences of what it had been like crossing the picket line for the first time. I was more certain than ever now that I had done the right thing.

The manager came in and gave us a welcome speech, telling us that we were helping to keep the pit open, he appreciated how hard it was for us to cross the picket lines. He reiterated that the strike was unofficial and that we weren't doing anything wrong. He went on to say that we were the best kind of mine worker and had ethics and morals that were to be admired.

I am pretty sure he meant it, but I couldn't help thinking it was just a rallying speech and well-rehearsed at that.

The police were walking about in the room with us and had shown some of the lads how to make truncheons with steel dowels down the middle, most of us carried one, myself included.

We got changed and got ready for going down the pit, there was no coal production at this stage, so we were on maintenance duties, such as greasing conveyor rollers and belt stitching. The pit deputies carried on working throughout as their union NACODS was not on strike, however some of them were hostile to us because they were sympathetic to the strike cause.

The shift went very quickly and whilst underground we had temporary respite from what awaits us on the surface.

Upon arriving back on the pit top we went into the baths we had to cross the road to get to the baths and of course that meant crossing the pickets again and enduring the hail of abuse that was thrown. We got back on the bus and yet again passed the pickets and headed off back home. Again there was a police van in front and one behind escorting the bus.

The bus dropped me off where it picked me up and luckily there was no pickets there, but others were not as lucky and had another barrage albeit on a smaller scale.

I was relieved to get inside to safety once again. I recounted the experience to my fiancée and her family, and I did feel relieved somewhat, however, there was a big downside and that was that it was not safe now for me to venture outside which meant I was a prisoner under house arrest as it were.

The news that night was full of the miners' strike as it had been for the previous six months, there were some very ugly scenes on the TV screen and a realisation of what may lie ahead.

The pattern remained the same the only difference was that each week there were more and more on the bus? One particular guy whose name I will not mention was on there who had been on the picket lines and had now joined us, not through choice mind you, he had been forced by his wife, he had been threatened with divorce if he didn't go back and start bringing some money in. He came back but was an absolute wreck, he was absolutely scared shitless. We didn't have any sympathy for him to be honest, only weeks before he had been one of the pickets hurling abuse and now he expected to be welcomed with open arms. It wasn't long however before he just couldn't take it and returned to the picket line. I am pretty sure he was planted to gather names of men that had returned for the union.

After a few weeks the manager asked us if any of us wanted to work in the number 1 shaft as a banksman, I volunteered and as I have had experience on the screens etc., he agreed for me to train up on that. I had now practically gone full circle and ended up back on the screens, but his time at the shaft side. My training was thorough but quick, I soon learned the ropes and just in time for coal production. The pit now had enough men to start producing coal again and before long we were up and running.

I was enjoying my new role, and the daily grind going through the picket line was by now a minor irritation, rather than something to dread. Don't get me wrong it still bothered me a little but the hurled abuse was now like water off a duck's back. I had even started venturing out catching a bus and going into Worksop. Life was near normal, or at least as normal as it could be. I was always armed with the truncheon that we made and I would have bloody well used it if needed.

I felt somewhat like a prisoner might feel being out on parole. I was constantly scanning my surroundings for anything that could possibly be trouble. I was always on edge.

This of course was the case for everybody that returned to work. We were all in the same boat.

There were numerous reports of working miners waving their wage packets at picket lines, this was categorically not the case at Whitwell, neither was it true that we were on double wages, this was as far as Whitwell was concerned total fabrication and propaganda. We did not get any perks, I did however ask the Manager if I could have a new tool belt and spanner which was granted. That would certainly have not been the case had we been not in strike conditions.

I watched the news constantly for developments, but it was the same scenes day after day. It was clear that the Yorkshire miners were the main instigators of trouble or least that was the way it was portrayed, Whitwell had its fair share of Yorkshire pickets, or flying pickets as they were known, and yes there was always trouble on the lines when they were present.

One particular incident at Whitwell was when pickets placed a wire across the road near Belph Bridge to bring a guy off his motor bike. They were caught and the management made it clear that if they were found guilty they would be dismissed.

One morning I woke up to go to work and noticed that the downstairs front room window had been put through and a lump of rock was in the middle of the floor. All damages would be paid for by the management this was made clear to us when we went back to work.

There was also a note shoved through the letterbox one day which was a death threat, this was handed to the police who were going to examine it forensically. My main concern there was that increased police and covert activities were supposed to be in place and if someone was able to post a note through the door it could just so easily have been a fire bomb.

My fiancée's parents were absolutely marvellous and supportive, it was clear that they did not go into this with their eyes closed. This did place some guilt on me somewhat, after all A few months ago they didn't even know me and now they are in the midst of a civil war with their property coming under attack from people in their own community. That did bother me, I felt that I had placed them in the firing line and lowered their standing in the community.

Fig 00012
Typical armoured bus used to ferry miner's through the picket line
Picture courtesy of David Devoy

Chapter 10

Behind Enemy Lines

As the weeks and months went by, getting on that bus as I said earlier was becoming very much easier, we became hardened to it, sure some guys couldn't hack it and returned to the picket lines. I can understand why that might be, it is not an easy thing to do at all, far from it. The guys that came back much later and had previously been on the picket lines soon had a strong realisation of how hard it was. From my point of view it was good for them to have a taste of what they had been dishing out for months. But again as I said earlier some guys who came back much later had no qualms about it at all and I strongly suspected them of being planted spies. The later guys too that came back after spending months hurling rocks and abuse at the buses, to me they were just hypocrites and the worst kind too, they were happy to hurl abuse and rocks with bravado and passion, but didn't much like it when they were on the receiving end. The original ones however were far from hypocritical, none of us had ventured anywhere near the picket lines. We had our opinion right from the start and were merely waiting for a national ballot, After all the fundamental right of the working man in this country is one man one vote, we were denied that right by the trade union that we had been funding for years, and furthermore were being dictated to by the same. So if you cannot vote by the ballot box then I for one will vote with my feet. The battle lines had been drawn and I and a good many others were crossing it. No ballot, No democracy, Equals, No strike, No rights. Simple equation, and I was the one who left school with no formal qualifications.

By now we decided that we needed some relief from the stress and to organise events outside of work and more importantly to get our women together so they could let their hair down so to speak. Let's not forget they were going through hell too, and were alone in some respects. They needed a release. We decided to arrange at least once a week to hire a bus to take us out to a pub somewhere for drinks and a bite to eat, but more importantly to forget the stress and anxiety and just relax with likeminded friends.

We decided on a pub in Scarcliffe in called the Horse and Groom. We were able to get our work driver on board and he drove the bus for us. These nights out were a welcome relief and the women enjoyed it immensely, as did we. The landlord at the time was more than happy for us to be there despite being surrounded by pits that were very much for the strike. We owed that man a debt of gratitude and we did show our appreciation at the time.

Before too long the strikers knew of our jaunt out and soon renamed Scarcliffe, "Scabcliffe". Quite funny I suppose. But this didn't alter things, we still continued and were still made welcome. We were well prepared for any trouble but luckily there wasn't any, luckily for them that is!

It was on one of these nights that I and my fiancée announced our intentions to get married in November which was only a few weeks away by now. The date had always been planned even before the strike, and I was concerned beforehand, if this was going to be possible. The lads and their wives and partners were all invited to the evening do. This was going to be. A big event, not the marriage as such but a wedding of a working miner in the village where the vast majority of residents were striking families. This sounded like a recipe for disaster, I know. We had to arrange this with the police of course and we did do that, they were aware of the date and time well beforehand. The week before on our usual visit to the Horse and Groom, the guys presented us with cards and gifts, one of these being a colour television. I had the biggest lump in my throat, I was clearly stunned that not only had they clubbed together to get these generous gifts but they had done so without me knowing anything about it, I didn't even suspect anything at all, this was a well-kept secret amongst them. I and my fiancée were overwhelmed by the kindness, the loyalty and the downright selflessness they had shown to us. These people were, ok, back at work but were not wealthy by any means, the strike had enforced it's harshness and financial pressures on them before they had returned to work, but they thought nothing of clubbing together for these gifts.

Well the wedding day was at hand, I was nervous, apprehensive, all the things that young men feel on their wedding day, but I had the added pressure of wondering if the day was going to pass smoothly and without incident. We headed off to the chapel in the village and we were driven by my very soon to be father in law. We rounded the corner to go down the narrow lane and all I could see were lots of police officers, bloody hell! They weren't here for the annual policeman's ball they were here to protect us at our wedding. The pipers who were originally friends of my fiancée and her family, were invited and they insisted on piping us into the chapel, this would draw attention at the best of times in sleepy Whitwell back then, let alone amongst the dozen or so police officers outside.

I remember after the service itself, I turned round and saw my work mates, they had braved venturing out to support us at our wedding, every one of them had turned up to that chapel, my first thought upon arrival at the chapel was that there would be more policemen at the wedding than guests, but now I could see all of them. This was a truly amazing fete, and I was quite choked to say the least, amongst the guests were my dear Grandma and my auntie grace, they had turned up to see me get married amongst all that police activity not knowing if it was going to turn out nasty or not. They were the only two that turned up from my side, obviously my dad wouldn't be there and to be honest I didn't want my mother there anyway. That may sound callous but what she put me through as a toddler was unforgivable and this was mine and my new wife's day and even if the strike had not happened she would not have been welcome.

The evening reception was to be in the scout hut, and there was no change to that. Before going to that me and my new wife wanted to visit my grandma at her home in her wedding dress, a small token of gratitude but it had to be done, my grandma had been a mother figure to me during my childhood and she more than made up for the lack of love from my mother, she was eighty eight years old yet she had made her own way to the chapel to see me wed. I thanked her for coming to the wedding, and she said that she was not going to miss that no matter what. She was glad that we took time out to visit her, my uncle however my dad's brother was not pleased to see me as he was a left winger too and supported the strike. I knew that beforehand but I wasn't going to let his thoughts about me stop me visiting my grandma.

We returned home to get ready for the evening do, we planned to go straight to the Temple hotel in Matlock Bath for the rest of the weekend after the evening do, then off to Cromer to spend a week with my wife's Sister.

At the evening reception, the pipers played traditional Scottish tunes on the bagpipes, this went down very well, the pipe major who did most of the playing bought lots of drinks for us and my mining friends, far from being a tight fisted Scots man that people typically associate Scots with, he was generous, and the miners loved him, he helped make the night, there's no doubt about that.

We set off to Matlock Bath and again my father in law drove us, my wife was still in her wedding dress, when we went up the steps to the hotel there was a woman sat on the steps, she said "have you just got married"? My normal sense of humour would have had a quip for a response but I declined the temptation. We checked in and all was well, the following morning I put on the television in the room, the news was on, and again it was full of the miner's strike, this time however, they were showing the burnt out wreck that used to be the strikers caravan very close to Whitwell pit. The newscaster said that arson was suspected. I was elated really, it was one up for us. It wasn't until later that I found out that it was some of my working miner friends after the wedding reception who attacked the caravan and raised it to the ground. This was a civil war in everybody's eyes so in view of the fact no one was hurt I was glad that we had struck back, they had their own way for far too long. We had suffered attacks on our personal property and endured months of horrific verbal abuse, so yes I couldn't be happier that we attacked them, and what better than to eliminate their own nerve centre. At least it wasn't on their personal property, we didn't terrorise women and children in their own homes by hurling rocks through the window in the dead of night like they did. We didn't make them prisoners in their own homes like they did us either. My wife had to give up her job in the knitwear factory because of the grief she was getting from the striking miners wives' who also worked there, so I think we were entitled to that attack.

After the weekend I went down to the hotel reception to check out, when the person on the desk told me that some journalists from a national newspaper had been enquiring as to whether I was staying there. She told me that it was against policy to confirm or deny who was residing in the hotel. She asked me if I was famous or something, when I told her she said that she couldn't understand all that stuff in the news and was sick of seeing it.

We left to go to Cromer in Norfolk to spend some time with my Sister and brother in law. Whilst we were there reporters were ringing daily to see if I would talk to them. I declined every time, low profile is the key and on honeymoon is not the stage to be making statements to the press about my working life. I suspected they wanted to interview me about the caravan of which I knew nothing about then anyway.

After the honeymoon was over we returned home to the stresses and strains of being a working miner again, I returned to work the following Monday morning and went through the usual barrage of abuse from the pickets, it was nerve racking again just like the first day, this was because I had had a break from it.

Since I had been away coal production was in full swing and as far as working was concerned life was normal again. This was a welcome relief and kept our minds off the stress we were suffering, the NUM was saying in the local news that Whitwell pit was not producing coal, the management was just winding the mineral shaft up and down to make it look like coal was being produced, although I can understand why they would think that. I was working on number 1 shaft which was the mineral shaft and it was definitely coal that was being emptied out of the skip and onto the plate belt, I know because I was the one shovelling half a ton of slack spillage every 30 minutes. That was definitely no propaganda exercise.

A few days later we had channel 4 news on site filming as coal was being brought to the surface, we found that a bit of an irritation but it did serve to prove that coal was being produced. Although I appeared on the film that they did I stayed out of their way.

Christmas was by now almost upon us, the NUM were predicting that power cuts would be in place by now, this was hardly likely, and there was a stock pile of coal that was the highest it had been for the past eleven years. The strike was called in the spring so energy requirements were always going to be less in the summer than in the winter. So obviously if you plan to bring the country to its knees and the government down, then calling a strike under the conditions above would ensure that it would be quite some time before the impact was really felt.

fig01011
Horse and Groom at Scarcliffe

CHAPTER 11

The political battle

As with all civil wars, politics has a big part to play. The miners' strike was no exception to this. Ones point of view depends very much on which side you're fighting for or vice versa I suppose.

I didn't take the side of the conservative government, I had my issues with the conservative government most notably the poll tax. I was on Â£86 per week and paying Â£158 per month in poll tax. It was crippling, it was not means tested and was not a fair system at all. I don't believe that the Tories set out initially to bring down the miners' union. I believe that the coal industry had to be modernised. If the government ever wanted to bring down the miners unions then they had their chance during the 1972 miners' strike. The miners then were demanding a 43% pay rise when the norm was between 6 and 8%. The difference then however was there was a national ballot and that ballot was in favour of strike action. The demands were unreasonable but nevertheless the vote was for strike action. The miners came out on strike and the NUM were compelled to accept a much smaller offer after balloting its members. That dispute resulted in over 130 pits being closed in Wales.

In 1984 The Tories wanted to close 20 pits to make the industry more economical, few pits were turning a profit, Whitwell hadn't made a profit in the previous twenty years. Arthur Scargill used this opportunity to try to bring down the government using the miners as his weapon of choice. I do not believe at all that he had the miner's interest at heart. His only goal was to parachute his way into Downing Street. If he was merely interested in fighting for jobs and preserving the pits then he would have done his homework first. The coal stocks were at an eleven year high. It was the start of spring, it was cheaper to import coal from Japan than it was to produce it in this country. Those reasons alone would tell you that the timing couldn't have been worse. Which of course is why he never held a national ballot, he knew there was no mood for strike action at least not all out strike action. By constantly denying his members of their right to a ballot only ensured that the strike would never be solid. Democracy is the key word here, men and women in past history have died fighting for democracy and here he was denying his own people of that hard fought right. The vast majority that went back to work at Whitwell and other pits did so for that reason and that reason only to defend that right.

Arthur Scargill of course is a left wing activist, just like my dad. Democracy is only applicable when it works in his favour. The moment it doesn't then he wouldn't use it, which is why when he was voted president he changed the ruling so that the job would be for life. Simple democracy was to him like the first stage in a space bound rocket, it is very useful whilst its power is propelling you forward, but the moment the power has gone and is of no further use to you, you discard it. Once it has been discarded it is nigh on impossible to get it back. But like that rocket first stage, you are never going to get anywhere without it in the first place. Scargill of course knew that, he might have been warped but he was not stupid. He was a very good orator, but the dictators have always been good orators they have had to be to drown out the voices of democracy. In view of what happened in 1972, twenty pits would have been the more sensible option and would have given the miners a stronger bargaining argument if the government tried closing more pits later. The job losses would have been minimal as there was a policy of transferring to nearby pits, redundancies in the first instance would have been from natural means such as early retirement. No one can argue today that the coal industry should have been sustained at pre-strike levels, Closures would have occurred naturally through exhaustion and geological conditions. The 12 month long strike did more to close pits than any government could have done. After the strike coal mines were disappearing at an alarming rate, and today there are only about eight collieries remaining out of about two hundred before the strike. Arthur Scargill in all honesty mismanaged the strike from the start. It is clear to me that the only reason for not calling a national ballot was purely and simply he could not be sure he would win it, so in true Marxist fashion he denied the national ballot to his members. One of the most heard chants on the picket lines was "The miners united will never be defeated" I believe that statement could very well be true, but the truth is The miners were not united, they were never likely to be without a national ballot, as I have said many times before the basic fundamental rule of trade unionism is One Man One Vote. Mrs. Thatcher, no matter what colour flag you fly, was no mug, she had planned in advance for this conflict, after previously backing down to the NUM in the 1981, and then the threat of strike action was enough to force a back down, primarily due to low coal stocks. As all armies that have had to retreat do so and then regroup and come back stronger, Scargill did nothing to prepare for this, maybe a labour government might have backed down again, who knows? If Scargill had played by the rules, rules that had been hard fought for by working men of all industries, then maybe, just maybe he would have been on a better wicket, he would have gained support from the other unions such as the steel workers and printing unions. Two miners from nearby Manton colliery took the NUM to court over the refusal to allow its members a national ballot, the high court ruled in favour of the miners from Manton stating that the NUM had breached its own constitution and fined both Scargill and the NUM. Scargill again played dirty and transferred the NUM's funds abroad to prevent them being sequestrated by the courts when he refused to pay the fine. Further evidence that democracy has no part in Arthur Scargill's life, it gets in his way. I have witnessed Marxism's tactics, they court favour by gaining trust, tell the people they have the answer to their problems, and then when they have obtained power the door to democracy is firmly bolted shut. He knew that if he shouted loudly enough he would be able to get someone to listen, he used his popularity to gain trust where that didn't work scare tactics were used.

I readily accept that there are differing views to the ones I have stated and that's how it should be. During the strike working miners were called Maggie's puppets, the truth of the matter is no working miner that I came across crossed the picket line in support of the government. We all did it in defiance for the refusal to a national ballot by the very union we had been paying for. Furthermore no miner who crossed the picket line would have crossed an official picket line brought about by a majority vote in a national ballot. That's democracy, like it or lump it we would have abided by the majority verdict. I know I speak for every working miner when I say that. When Nottinghamshire miners voted regionally 20,000 out of 27,000 miners voted against strike action, Scargill's response was to threaten them with expulsion, yet another example of democracy being disregarded by Scargill. Then when the Nottinghamshire miners started their own union the UDM (Union of Democratic Mineworkers) he reviled that too, but in reality he was the orchestrator of it, it came about simply because the Nottinghamshire miners were threatened with expulsion from the NUM and that would leave them without any recourse, so what were they supposed to do? Scargill in my view is a buffoon, his mismanagement of the whole thing led the miners to defeat, and he did the government's job for them.

The tory government made it possible for miners to cross the picket line in relative safety, at the end of the day they didn't have to do that, the strike was illegal, and realistically we could have been dismissed for frustration of contract. I recognise that by providing resources to enable us to cross the picket line suited the government just as much as it did us.

The best way to keep coal mines open is to work them and make them profitable, not abandon them for a whole year. I heard NUM members on the TV saying that the government was trying to close the pits purely on economic grounds, apart from geological conditions and exhaustion there is no better reason for closing pits. I would defy anybody today to run a business that runs at a loss. It just doesn't make sense. The industrial world was changing and the coal mines like the rest of the country would have to change with it.

There are many victims of civil war and industrial disputes, with industrial disputes the biggest victims always is the general public, all strikes of national industries and public service industries always hold the governments to ransom by harming its people, whether that be by not emptying the bins, running the trains, fighting the fires, healing the sick, the list is endless but it is always the ordinary man and woman on the street that suffers. Nobody in their right mind would go into a school yard and bully and intimidate a school child to get its father to give in to his demands, silly analogy I know but when you think about it, it's exactly like that with industrial disputes. With the miners' strike I remember seeing a curly haired young strike supporter saying he longed for Christmas to come and the lights go out through depleted energy stocks. So he would be happy to ruin a child's Christmas to further his own demands on the government, it was bad enough they were ruining their own children's Christmas by not being able to afford Christmas presents.

The claim by Scargill that the Tories were out to decimate the coal industry was totally false. The truth is that under Harold Wilson's labour government nearly two hundred and fifty coal mines were closed and with the agreement of the unions, whilst Mrs. Thatcher's conservative government closed one hundred and fifty. I am pretty convinced that had the strike not taken place then it would have been far less than one hundred and fifty. Of course Scargill and his followers wouldn't want you to remember those facts. As I have said before, Arthur Scargill decimated the coaling industry, coal mines were on a knife edge with regards to viability and not working them for one whole year only served to hasten the demise of the mines. You simply cannot lock the doors of a coal mine like a factory.

Miners on both sides of the divide were indeed pawns, I and my fellow working miners were to a degree pawns of the government, I do accept that to some degree, but the striking miners were definitely pawns of Arthur Scargill. We were the soldiers in the respective armies. It is a travesty that we have lost our coal mines and the heritage that went with them, I, although biased, do lay the blame for that firmly at Arthur Scargill's door. He finished the mines and the miners off.

Arthur Scargill was a member of the young communist league, he joined that in nineteen fifty five. There is no place in modern British politics for communism.

One absolutely laughable dictat of Arthur Scargill came in 2012 when he demanded that the NUM continued paying £34000 per annum for a flat in London for the rest of his life and any widow who survived him, more amazingly the £34000 was being paid without the ordinary NUM member's knowledge or approval. Communism at work indeed. Communists do not believe in democracy at all. They think that people power should only be heard when it's in support of them, once that support is no longer needed, then oppression is the order of the day.

Better people than Arthur Scargill had tried to bring down Governments and failed. The arrogance of the man just epitomises the practices of the Marxist movement, promise all the people everything and talk in a language that sounds logical to the average working man, but in reality once in power all democratic rights would be removed. The world we would come to know would be far removed from what we have now, there would be no home ownership, no personal wealth, no supermarkets, no car ownership, and no cash in your pocket only vouchers. The list is endless. Needless to say we would be in an oppressed state where the right to free speech would not exist. Luckily the British people have more sense than that and would in my opinion never elect for that kind of life. I know the Governments of the day in this country are far from transparent but the alternative just doesn't bear thinking about. Without the fear of repeating myself Arthur Scargill is a great orator, shouting at the top of his voice, this is a common practice of dictators throughout history. The thing I hate and detest most about the man is that he used the mine workers as his army of choice believing them to be capable of ousting the government, he used them for his own political ends only to cast them aside when it was all over, leaving the miners to pick up what little remained of the mining industry. To this day I long for a one to one face to face confrontation with him. He has an awful lot to answer for he set man against man, Father against son, Neighbour against neighbour and most of he tried to kill democracy in this country that many men and women throughout history had lost their lives trying to defend.

I believe that every man woman and child has a right to his or her views and that those views should be respected, we are all individuals with individual ideologies. Just because one person doesn't agree with another doesn't mean that that person is wrong and has to be dictated to. I have said many times before that democracy is the key in this country it has proven itself to work time and time again. If Scargill had held a national ballot and if that ballot was for strike action then like it or lump I and everyone else who crossed the picket lines would be out on strike no question of doubt in my mind whatsoever. I and the countless others that crossed the picket lines did so in the name of democracy not in the name of Mrs. Thatcher or the Tory Government and certainly not just to keep a wage coming in, remember the old adage "United we stand – Divided we fall" Absolutely true. The Miners themselves on the picket lines were singing the infamous "The Miners – United Will never be defeated" If only they had stopped and listened to the words of the song they were singing then maybe just maybe they would have kicked Scargill into touch and demanded a national ballot. If you believe differently to me then I absolutely respect that, it is your right as it is mine to hold that view.

There are many faults with all governments who are elected in to power, the answer to those failings will never be communism in this country, and the British people are too intelligent for that.

Should any doubt be cast about communism, I will finish off by explaining the relevance of my dedicating so much of this chapter to it. Communist writers and thinkers believe that the world should be a classless society where nobody owns property, the people should work in exchange for the things they need to survive. There is no money in a communistic society. They fail to say how people will survive in retirement when they are no longer able to work, the people own everything because there is no state, but in reality of course they own nothing, freedom of speech is not welcome or tolerated in communism. My last word here for Arthur Scargill is that the coal mines are represented by the pick and shovel not the hammer and sickle.

CHAPTER 12

The end of the Strike

The daily grind of going through the picket line lasted for a long six months, I did find it easier as time went on and going through the barrage of angry pickets became second nature by now. My wife and I were living with her parents, we were committed to buying our house in Whitwell but had arranged with the vendor and the mortgage company to wait until the strike was over before completing the sale. Luckily for us the housing market was depressed and the vendor had no other offers to consider.

Christmas 84 was soon upon us, my thoughts were of the miners kids that would be missing out this year, more innocent victims of Scargill's crusade. Christmas at our house was a little low key but enjoyable nonetheless. I am lucky that I wasn't a drinker because going out in the village drinking would have been totally out of the question.

The news as always was full of tales of woe from the picket lines, true there was genuine hardship for some families but they had the same choice as the rest of us, they were inflicting hardship on their families and I can only reiterate I felt sorry for the kiddies that would be going without, after all, Christmas is for the kids. So along came the new year 1985 had dawned, the sound of "auld Lang sine" being sung on the TV, wishing each other a happy new year, but I knew that it was going to be far from a happy new year this year, I had little doubt about that. I couldn't help but wonder what the year was going to bring.

The holiday was over and back to groundhog day, the same early morning routine, only difference was that there was a few more new faces on the bus, for me that was good, the best ending for this is that they all eventually trickle back but in reality that was never going to be the case, but the more that came back the better it would be.

Coal production at Whitwell pit was in full production by now, and as I said striking miners were trickling back thick and fast too. I found it surreal that these men had spent ten months on the picket lines only to return to work before the end of the strike. I couldn't help but wonder what the point of that was. Some of the miners that returned were obviously being standoffish with us and refusing to speak, I remember one guy coming to the shaft side of number one shaft that I was working at, I went to let him onto the cage and just passed the time of day with him. I knew he had been a hard liner on the picket lines but I didn't see the point of holding that against him, especially since he had done the same thing as us albeit some months later. Nevertheless he had crossed the picket line so that made him the same as us. He ignored me totally, He slapped his tally into my hand in a manner that meant it bounced out onto the floor. (Me) "What the fuck's your problem"?

(Miner)   "You don't really need me to tell you that do you? You scabby bastard"

(Me)   "Well the last time I fuckin looked the strike was still on, and you are here on this side of the fence, so what the fuck does that meck you"?

(Miner)   "A tha calling me a fuckin scab?"

(Me)   "Well if the cap fits fuckin wear it, but tha aint gooin no weer until thas picked up that tally".

By this time the phone in my cabin was ringing. I answered it and it was the winder in the winding house.

(Winder)   "What's the hold up? A tha ringin cage down or what"?

(Me)   "Ave got a clever cunt givin me grief"

(Winder)   "As tha indeed, does tha need any elp"?

(Me)   "No al be allrate, but he aint gooin no fuckin weer wi that attitude, talk about pot calling kettle black".

I went back to the shaft side and the miner was still stood there but he had picked up the tally.

(Miner) "A tha gunna let me goo darn or what"?
(Me)   "That's up to thee mate, but I aint tekkin no fuckin lip from yo, if tha puts the tally in me and rate tha can goo but not until"

He walked up to me and placed the tally in my hand a little firmly then walked onto the cage. I rang the signal and off he went. If that is the treatment from him what is going to be like when the rest come back after the strike, one thing for sure it's going to be awkward at the very least, and to be honest I always knew that.

Subsequent shifts were better but very frosty when dealing with long term strikers that had come back to work, it was clear that they didn't regard themselves as strike breakers or scabs as we had become known as. They didn't seem to get any problems from the pickets either, they were able to walk through the village without too much bother. I too by this stage was venturing out into the village and the local town of Worksop, I passed a few striking miners on the streets but only got verbal abuse when there was more than one of them, never when they were on their own, it seems that was the same for my work mates. Things weren't that great for my wife however as she was getting some stick at work from the miners wives that worked there, when she raised this with her bosses she was told that she was very much in the minority and it may be best if she left. She ended up resigning. The attitude was abhorrent really and would not be tolerated in today's society. Industrial tribunals would have a field day.

Opinion polls were being carried out with the general public and it was clear from these that the longer the strike went on the less public support there was for it, a few results that I had noted at the time are as follows.

July 1984 40% for the coal board; 33% were for the miners. 19% were for neither and 8% don't know's

December 1984, 51% for the coal board; 26% were for the miners; 18% were for neither and 5% don't know's

Similar results were obtained regarding the tactics used by striking miners. Die hard Scargill supporters were beginning to lose faith in him too.

By the end of February Scargill attended yet more talks to find a settlement, it was at these talks that Scargill eventually gave in, and ordered his men back to work, It is unclear what made him give in but it would be interesting to find out. The miners waiting outside were not happy and were singing" we're not going back – we're not going back". He gave in after 2 people lost their lives during the strike, one guy died on the picket line outside Ollerton Colliery, he was hit by a brick. Police were not in the habit of throwing bricks so it must have been by one of the pickets. Similarly a taxi driver was killed by two striking miners who dropped a concrete post on his taxi whilst he was taking a working miner into the pit in South Wales. These incidents did nothing to curry favour with the general public. These and the fact that power stations had more than enough reserves of coal to supply the country with electricity throughout the winter helped to hasten the demise of the strike and indeed the NUM itself.

So after one whole year exactly the strike was over, the miners were to return to work on Tuesday 5th March which is a year to the day of the strike starting. 27 million workin day's lost. As far as the country at large was concerned it was over and everything was to get back to normal. In reality it was far from normal and far from over. Some miners stayed out in support of miners that had been dismissed through their actions on the picket lines, these were the die hards.

I remember the day they came back vividly. We waited with bated breath for their return on the morning of March 5th. They came marching down the road from the bridge proudly holding the NUM banner aloft, anyone who didn't know better could easily think that they had won the battle. The striking miners said they came back with their tales between their legs. I for one think they were quite magnanimous in defeat.

We were expecting trouble from the outset and were well prepared for that, however it was a quiet if not disappointing return. They didn't just roll over and play dead though, there were quite a few snide remarks from many of them. I was stood in the canteen area when they came marching in and I received a few choice looks I can tell you. Amazingly however there was not one comment. I thought then that at last this whole sorry year long ordeal was now over. I didn't see my father amongst them but I know he would have been there.

I was lucky in some respects, I was working on number one shaft, the man riding shaft is number two. A few of us decided to call in at number two shaft to give our colleague some support as he would be facing them all alone. I stood there with the banksman and I could hear a lot of under breath comments which I chose to ignore. We as a team of working miners had decided to ignore choice remarks unless they were aimed directly or could cause unsafe scenes at the shaft side. We decided to play it the way I did earlier, hence anyone slapping their tallies or flicking them at us would not go underground until they had behaved properly. As the banksman put his hand out for the tallies off the men as they entered the cage there were indeed some forceful pressing of the tallies into his hand along with choice stare's, but nothing to really make an issue of. There was a few louder remarks once they started going down the shaft and these echoed in the shaft walls.

I went off to man number one shaft, which was adjacent to the screens. The screens workers were on station and most of them had been on strike throughout. My cabin was all windows to enable a complete view of the shaft area, this also meant that I would see the screens workers as they went to and from their cabin, I had worked with these guys when I worked on the screens before going underground. I did red receive a few choice looks from some of them but got absolutely no verbal remarks at all. If I joined them in their cabin at snap times some of them would just not look or speak, but to be honest that was to be expected and it didn't really affect me.

March passed relatively smoothly and was not as bad as expected, bad blood was still evident and of course there was always the odd snide remark. My old foreman came into the shaft cabin on one particular shift, I wondered how he would react, he was quite pleasant really and although standoffish when he spoke he did so with respect. One particular morning shift there was a problem at number two shaft which meant the miners had to enter the pit through number one shaft which of course was my shaft. There was a couple of hundred men lining up at my shaft which meant that there would be eight or nine runs. I obviously had to stand at the shaft cage entrance to open the cage curtains to let them on. Comments were plentiful I can tell you, I could never pinpoint which ones were making the remarks but it was blatantly clear they were aimed at me, I did try to ignore them but it was hard. As soon as they started to board the cage we had the usual tally tossing. I had to stop proceedings and then I took a deep breath and said to the miners waiting.

(Me) "Anybody that flicks or tosses their tally and not put them in my hand will not go down the pit at this shaft, I will refuse to allow passage under the mines and quarries act".

There were a few mutterings but it did the trick, although the tallies were placed in my hand with more force than usual I could live with that. Once in the cage and descending into the mine they found their voice again, quite laughable really looking back now.

One Month after the end of the strike me and my wife completed the long awaited contract to purchase our first house in Whitwell, It was by sheer fluke that the guy next door was a working miner and was the banksman at number two shaft. This helped as we also had an extra pair of hands to help with the move.

Not long after settling in I was contacted by ITV asking if I would do an interview on the strike, they had cottoned on to the father son situation. I refused at this point because I didn't want to dwell on the topic, I was looking to repair the damage the strike had caused and I didn't think that a TV interview would help in that regard. There was another incident earlier involving a well-known TV breakfast show that ended up with me and a well-known NUM leader having a slanging match in the green room, and that interview was scrapped, the TV Company refused to allow reference here to that attempted interview.

Towards the end of the strike my brother came up to my in-laws house to inform me that my dad had suffered another heart attack and he was wanting me to visit. I obviously went to see him and although quite frosty he seemed happy to see me. I was beginning to think that he was coming round. Soon after he went home I went to visit him again at his home, it was on one of these visits my mother informed me that when I was younger they had taken out an insurance policy, as they did with both me and my Brother. The policy was for just over £300. After I signed it they made it blatantly clear that I wasn't welcome and nothing had changed and not to go round anymore. I was shaking with rage, not so much of the con but that my dad could stoop to such levels. It wasn't the money either they had paid it in, it was theirs as far as I was concerned. But not bad tactics to say he was against capitalism, it seems only other people aren't allowed to make money. Although I was angrier than I had ever been I couldn't get violent with him because he was my dad at the end of the day and no matter what you cannot go round hitting your own father. By the same token one wouldn't expect a father to do that to his son. The bitterness that caused still remains with me even today.

CHAPTER 13

After the Strike

April 1985 saw us moving into our first house together, things were as normal as they could be, the battle bus was no longer in use and we were walking to the pit as before. One particular day however I was walking through the village on my way to start an afternoon shift when there was a couple of miners just coming out of the pub. I had made a conscious decision that I was not going to walk with my head down or cross over the road, I had done nothing to be ashamed of. So I carried on, as I passed by one of them muttered "scab". I thought well ok then there are two of them they have been drinking, let it go. I knew both of them and the one who made the remark lived on pit row and was a close friend of my dad's. I walked a bit further and he repeated his remark a little bit louder.

"Scab"

(Me)   "I fuckin rich cumin from thee, the idlest bastard in fuckin pit, biggest work shy fucker out there"

(Miner) "A tha talking to me"?

(Me)   "Am fuckin looking at thee so I must be talking to thee"?

This time the guys mate that was with him told him to back off and leave it, he's looking for a fight and I rise to the cunt he said.

(Miner) "Ahh ees not fuckin woth it, even his father dunt want owt to do WI the cunt".

They both then crossed over the road and went into a nearby store. Truth is I wasn't looking for trouble, far from it, I had to respond because if I didn't it would just have escalated every time we passed in the street. It was lucky that he didn't push it, I was carrying my truncheon and by god I would have used it to defend myself, this guy was well known by everybody as being very work shy, and to be honest bone idle. I what bothered me really, the strike probably suited him as it gave him a year off. His mate was known for being able to handle himself, but I knew he wasn't a trouble maker. The guy's remark about my dad though did bother me not least because it was true. It was another situation whereby remarks are only made when they are not on their own, I don't think it's because they have back up, I think it's more to do with bravado and looking big in front of your mates by acting the big hard man. In normal circumstances the ordinary man in the street would just ignore it and not rise to it. I couldn't afford to do that, not that I want trouble because that was the last thing I want, but I had endured six months of hell along with my colleagues to enforce a democratic right, if I just carried on walking and ignore this type of behaviour, that would make them think that I was guilty as charged as it were, I have to stand up for myself, I didn't go through all that abuse from the picket lines to appear to be ashamed of it

Incidents like that though, thankfully, are few and far between, nevertheless it happened from time to time. It was clear though that not all of us who broke the strike got that sort of abuse in the street, mostly they were just ignored.

My wife told me that she was in the street shopping when my dad was walking up the other side of the road, she said he called her a Bastard. That to me was very uncharacteristic of him, I know he has warped political beliefs from my perspective but I found it hard to believe he would hurl language like that across the street, after all, as kids we never ever heard him use foul language at home. I heard him use it down the pit, I can remember being very shocked the first time I heard him use the F word.

But these were abnormal times and he has behaved out of character in a lot of ways in the last year, so there could be truth in what she said.

At the pit there was a lot of down time as far as production of coal was concerned, one breakdown after another, it transpired that electrical supply cables were being cut deliberately. These cables to give you a picture were very sizeable, some of them being a lot thicker than the standard domestic drain pipes. This was the next tactics it seemed of the ex-striking miners to cause disruption to the pits ability to function. This behaviour is absolute madness, the whole point of the year long strike was too allegedly fight to keep pits open, my view was that the only way to keep pits open was to work them. The strike caused damage to the pits economic viability as it was, although the wage bill was vastly reduced due to the miners' strike action, they still lost a huge amount of money. It was said that Whitwell colliery actually turned a profit during the strike once coal production restarted. Further hindering the mines ability to function by vandalism with a full contingent of miners, only served to hasten the mines demise. If this behaviour was not unique to Whitwell, then the coal mining industry would not survive. This is just another explanation of the miners doing the government's job for them. It was a self-destructive path they were heading down, not to mention putting men's lives at risk. The more sensible approach would be to go all out to boost production to help prove that the pit was an economic viability, which in turn would make it harder for the Government to close the pit purely on economic grounds.

As with all strikes there is never any winners, the miners' strike was no different, the miners lost out on a year's work, their families lost out on the basic necessities in life, and the coal board lost out by having more pits than ever being uneconomical and most would be unrecoverable. The tax payer lost out by having to fund resources to keep the peace and keeping our roads open etc. If there was a winner it was the government.

Production at Whitwell never again reached pre-strike levels and the pit was rapidly becoming unsustainable or more unsustainable to be precise. Cost of producing coal by now was £69 per ton and the selling price was £42. Leading to a loss over approximately eight million pounds in the year following the strike.

There were still many vandalism instances mainly underground, one man who returned to work even had needles inserted into his soap, resentment was running high on both sides. It was clear that we all had to watch our backs more than ever, we all got into the practice of checking our lockers and equipment with more scrutiny.

I still helped out my old friend Frank Bird at weekends, he had his views on the strike and they differed from mine, however he never let the differences and my breaking the strike interfere with our friendship, we discussed it many times but always agreed to differ. I the way it should be, I have always accepted that other people will have views that differ to mine and I have always respected that, even, believe it or not throughout the strike. I don't think that relationships should be ruined on a mere difference of opinion. In a democracy views from all side are taken and the views and wishes of the majority are taken, that's exactly how it should be. Whenever a political will is dictated then conflict always ensues, the miners' strike was a prime example of that.

Frank was always friendly with my father through his relationship with me mostly, but Frank was friendly with everybody no matter who they were. This relationship often meant that dad would be round at Frank's when I was there and vice versa which meant for very frosty encounters. I always had a resentment of him and no doubt the same was true with him for me, the difference was that despite everything I always wanted to, and tried to, repair the relationship, each approach I made was rebuffed. That not only saddened me but hurt, the same is true even today some thirty years on.

Production at Whitwell never again reached pre-strike levels and the pit was rapidly becoming unsustainable or more unsustainable to be precise. Cost of producing coal by now was £69 per ton and the selling price was £42. Leading to a loss over approximately eight million pounds in the year following the strike.

The rest of the 1985 continued to improve very slightly, I was getting very little grief now from the ex-striking miners with a few exceptions. In September of that year my wife fell pregnant, pretty ironic almost a year to the day since I went back to work. The prospect of becoming a father myself for the first time focussed my mind somewhat. I knew that if things didn't improve where my dad was concerned then he was going to miss out on his first Granddaughter. I was absolutely adamant that no matter what happened between me and my dad my mother would never get the chance to be a proper grand Mother. Sure, I would let her see her but there would be no chance what so ever of sleep over's or babysitting, I would never expose any child of mine to being left alone with an evil woman such as her. Life from now on would take another change but this time it would be a happier one, and of course I did wonder if my going back to work would impact on her life.

November saw our first wedding anniversary, a difficult year had passed and had put a strain on our marriage. We had to now focus on getting a room ready for our baby daughter that was due the following June. I couldn't help wonder how many couples have had such a difficult first year of married life. Most couples would have a year of love and romance, we never had time for that as such, but we had survived a difficult courtship and first year so there was hope for the future. My in-laws made a big thing of our first year as a married couple, my father in law was a very proud of me and took every opportunity to tell me so. He had taken the blame for me going back to work by my dad and a few others, he found this laughable, he told me that it wasn't him getting the blame that bothered him it was more that the people were assuming I wasn't capable of making that decision on my own. I told him that I wouldn't have been able to make that decision without his support. He put his hand on my shoulder and said" Steve I am proud to know you, I am proud that you are my son in law but more importantly I am proud that you trusted me to help you with what was a monumental decision, you have turned your back on not only 90% of the mining community, but your family. With a few exceptions like your grandmother and your brother, you didn't give in to your dad's dictatorial advice or the mob rule. You knew what you would be going into when crossing that picket line, I never saw you dither once. A young man that you are and have had all this to cope with as well as buying your first home, getting married and now expecting your first child. All we have done is be there for you when you needed us to be. You have had one hell of a 18 month period with stress levels beyond compare, I am not sure I could have done that, it took guts and your dad should be proud that you were strong enough to act upon what you believed in. But to be honest in my opinion your dad doesn't deserve to have a son with scruples, intelligence, morals and above all a backbone".

(Me) "Wow, that has brought a lump to my throat, but I don't think it brave as such more stubbornness. I was determined that I was wasn't going to be dictated to by a Marxist union leader who doesn't believe his members have a right to vote, the rule book says there will be a national ballot before any industrial action, he knew that he wouldn't get a majority vote for strike action so he made it an area vote. He shouts loud like the dictator that he is and uses his bully boys from Yorkshire to force his will across the country. His only aim is to topple the tory government and to instil himself in government. He is a devout Marxist, he is a cancer who will let nothing or anybody stand in his way, and he is riding on the back of the Labour party because that is the only hope of getting anywhere near power. Once labour get in him will take over the party, I have no doubt about that. So I am not brave I just know what's right and what's wrong, the strike had been judged illegal therefore staying away from work was breaking my contract because there was no mandate for a strike".

In reality I suppose it does appear brave from the outside, and in some ways it was. Crossing a picket line is not an easy thing to do, not easy at all, you have to be very sure of yourself and do it with your eyes open. Then pluck up the courage. You need the support of the people around you because your decision will always affect them.

CHAPTER 14

The first anniversary of the end of the strike

It was now 1986 Christmas had come and gone and the anniversary of the end of the strike is looming large, I came home from the pit one night after an afternoon shift and my wife said that TVAM had been on the phone wanting to do an interview, I was reluctant after the charade of the earlier episode which resulted in a cancellation, not saying it was TVAM but it was a TV company, they are embarrassed at that and will not allow me to go into details or name them. My wife said they would phone me back in the morning.

The following Morning I awoke about 7am and got up, whilst awaiting for the kettle to boil the phone rang. I answered it.

(Me)   "Hello"
(Caller) "Hello is that Stephen Whyles"
(Me)   "Yes"
(Caller) "My name is Peter Van Gelder, I am a reporter for the ITV breakfast show TVAM, and I was wondering if you would do a TV interview at your home with regard to the miner's Strike"?
(Me)   "Not sure, the strike is now over"

(Peter) "Yes I know but 5th March is the first anniversary since the strike ended and we wanted to interview a cross section of the mining community, but your story is unique, what with the relationship with your dad"

(Me) "Have you contacted my dad then"?

(Peter) "Yes we have"

(Me) "Ok I can manage that"

(Peter) "Excellent, I will be there sometime next week, preferably Tuesday as the interview will be screened on Wednesday 5th".

(Me) "I am on days so it will have to be in the afternoon and I have a rest day on Wednesday anyway"

(Peter) "Not a problem I will see you about 4pm on Tuesday"

(Me) "Ok see you then".

I was a little unsure that it would be a good idea, but he said he had been in contact with my dad and I am buggered if I am going to let him spout off without a reply so I have to put my side across, It will either draw us closer together or distance us further. The relationship couldn't get any worse than it is now anyway.

My wife reminded me that I had gone through hell over the past 2 years effectively, my dad had disowned me, and she was right it was high time the public got my version of events.

The Morning of the 4th March came along, I did my days shift then went home as normal, about 3:45pm two black Range Rover cars pulled up outside, unmarked, 3 guys got out and started offloading equipment. I let them in and whilst the camera crew were setting up peter went through the questions he would be asking.

I asked Peter if he had spoken to my dad and he said that he was going there next. He had already done some filming in the village. His main interest centred around my joining the UDM, as I was only one of 18 UDM members at Whitwell, the relevance there was that the UDM was a primarily a Nottinghamshire union and Whitwell of course is in North Derbyshire. As it turned out my dad had refused to speak to them. Quite strange that, he had a perfect opportunity to put his point across and his political stance also. I was asked about my Mother and what her opinion was, I told him that I would not discuss my mother at all. The reason for that is I could easily stray into the abuse side of it and she would not have anything to say that would be useful in my opinion anyway. Had she joined in, I would have intimated at the reasons for her remarks being so negative, I think she knew that all along. I was careful throughout not to hint at the abuse because the media would have a field day on that. My view was that it was between me and her and I didn't want it broadcasting to the nation. The split between me and my dad would suit her in more ways than one, firstly she was getting what she wanted since I was born and that was me out of her life, secondly and more importantly it meant she wouldn't have to explain herself to me. I had always had every intention of getting answers from her.

The interview ended and I was reasonably happy with what had been discussed. I had thought that would be the end of the media and press interest in me, but because of the situation with me and my dad it clearly attracted media attention. TVAM was to be the first of many interviews it would seem.

The following morning I waited with bated breath for the piece to be broadcast. Anne Diamond was on the sofa with Nick Owen and guest Anne Leslie. They started the introduction and then played the interview. They spoke afterwards saying that they couldn't understand how families could be split over a political point of view. Anne Leslie went on to say how Arthur Scargill was an arrogant man and had mismanaged the strike from the start and was the cause of all the family and community break ups. The TV piece was rather short compared to the amount of film and interview they shot, but I suppose that was for editing purposes. I still have a copy of the interview today.

That evening I went to my UDM meeting at Creswell colliery, the members the meeting organisers mentioned the film I did and said how pleased they were with what I had said. The disappointment I had with it was that they never showed the clip where I told them how I thought that Arthur Scargill by refusing to give a national ballot had caused the divide in the village and more importantly the divide with my dad. My colleagues at the meeting said that they wouldn't be interested in that, they were only interested in the human impact, they are only keen to highlight that my dad had disowned me over a political decision. Furthermore they thought that my dad had dropped a clanger by not being interviewed because now he will have come across as the guilty and perhaps ashamed party in all of this. The TV reporter Peter made much about my wife being heavily pregnant and that the baby was due in two months' time, he asked me if I would allow my parents to see the child, I stopped the interview and told him to concentrate on my dad with no reference to my mother. He rephrased the question accordingly, initially I said no because that would be tantamount to abuse. I then stopped and asked him to do that bit again. He once again rephrased the question and I told him that I had hoped that my dad would come round perhaps not to my way of thinking but to agree to disagree then we could get back to being a father and son again and of course that would entail him seeing his Granddaughter. When the interview was aired they used the bit that said I wouldn't allow him to see his Granddaughter. I was very annoyed at that because it was not what I wanted putting across, Peter knew that and told me it would be discarded. They used the piece in my view to get maximum impact. I vowed then to never do anymore interviews for the ITV, which to this day I still haven't despite numerous requests from them. I was misrepresented but I blame myself because I did say that initially, lesson learned if you don't want anything broadcast that you don't believe then don't say it.

On returning to the pit the following day, I got quite a few stares and a few remarks, one guy came up to me in the baths as I was getting changed to start work and said.

"A suppose tha thought tha wo fuckin clever trying to meck thi dad look a cunt on national TV"

- (Me) "What the fucks that got to do wi thee what I say to any fucker, fuck off and keep thi nooas art on stuff that is none of your fuckin business"
- (Miner) "Dunt get arsey wi me, am just sayin what every fucker else is thinking".
- (Me) "well theres only thee sayin owt, if my dad or anyone else as a problem wee it then I couldn't give a flyin fuck to be honest, an apart from owt else ee add is chance to put his side an ee dint, so tha can tell im that, it's obvious he sent ya"
- (Miner) "Ees not bothered, ee ses that tha no son of his anyway". At that he left.

That statement he made last off really got to me, if I didn't know before I certainly knew now that this rift is going to be a long time in healing, if ever. I hinged my hope on the passage of time being a great healer and that eventually he would come round, surely nobody can be that stubborn indefinitely, can they?

Whatever the future would hold, I was certain that I wasn't going to be the one who prevented the relationship from being repaired, however, the longer we remained estranged I suppose, the harder it will be. It seems that the general consensus in the village went against anybody making comments that did nothing to resolve the differences, I remember being in the local co-op when a woman who was shopping told me that she thought I was foolish going back to work but thought my dad was wrong to say the things he did about me in the paper. I knew the woman was married to a staunch strike supporter. With that I at least knew that my dad would lose favour if he continued with the remarks.

Back at the pit there was rumours circulating regarding the future of a lot of coal mines, this fuelled speculation that Whitwell pit would also close. It wasn't until the 3rd of June until the fate of Whitwell pit would be known, it was indeed going to close after losing eight million pounds in the year following the strike. In my view the strike that was held to prevent closures of coal mines had only served to hasten the closures of the ones earmarked and added a few more to the list due to the unviability. You simply cannot leave a coal mine unworked for a whole year and expect it to survive, once a pit is closed it is nigh on impossible to reopen it.

Arthur Scargill was making fresh calls for strike action, these calls went unanswered by his members. That call just epitomised Scargill's lack of feeling for his own members. They had just endured a whole year of hardship on his say so having faith that he would win the dispute. They have not recovered yet from that year of striking and he expected them to down tools and strike again, it just reinforces the guy's lack of feeling and understanding for his own men, they had no fight left in them.

Voluntary redundancies were being offered by the coal board, offerings of £1000 per year worked, at the time that was a good offer bearing in mind that they could quite easy have gone for compulsory redundancies. I went to see the pit Manager and asked if I would be able to transfer to Creswell Colliery which was not only close geographically but was in the Nottinghamshire coal field so I would be among friends. The Manager refused using the old rule of not being able to transfer out of the area, it would have to be a Derbyshire coal field. After discussing this with my wife I decided that I would opt for redundancy.

And leave the industry. I knew that by leaving the industry altogether would not leave the legacy that the strike had caused behind. The mine shafts were destroyed in 1987 bringing to an end the existence of Whitwell Colliery after a 96 year history, I feel strongly that if the strike had not occurred the pit would have survived its Centenary. Well done Arthur Scargill.

Fig 09 Whitwell Colliery site 1986
Picture courtesy of Phil Sangwell

Fig 10 Whitwell Colliery site 2013

CHAPTER 15

Life after the pit

June 1986 saw a new beginning for me in more ways than one, I had now left the pit for good and I was now a proud father of my daughter Natalie. I had found a job as a domestic appliance engineer in Tuxford. I started working for a company that repaired Bosch, Neff and Siemens appliances. I had a knack of repairing washing machines and the like from a young age. After a comprehensive training programme with the German's I was set to start on the road in a new career entirely. The life of a coal miner seemed worlds away from this line of work. Due to the high class nature of the appliances, I would be visiting the homes of people I would class as upper class, the ones that talked with a plum in their mouth. The biggest learning curve here was talking to them without the Derbyshire dialect. I spent quite a lot of time in London with training etc., A lot of my usual working would be based in and around south Nottingham especially West Bridgeford, Rufford park was a favourite too. One incident I remember vividly was a customer on Rufford park estate. I had nine calls to make but five were AM calls four of which were in Sheffield S10. Rufford Park, AM was classed as before 1pm for some strange reason, anyhow I finished the four calls in Sheffield but one was a bearing change which held me up somewhat. I headed down to Rufford and got there about ten past two. The woman came out as I parked up and said

"Where have you been young man? You should have been here at 1 o'clock.

(Me)   "Why what happened"?

(Customer) "How dare you? You insolent young man one does not call for an engineer to call over an hour after one was expecting, and certainly not one that has no respect for his clientele. I will report you to your superior, and you can wait just there and get off my property".

(Me)   "Sorry madam, one wasn't expecting to get held up in Sheffield prior to one calling here, but stay here or get off your property which is it to be? One has other customers to attend to you know"

(Customer) "Ooh I should give you a seeing to, back chatting me in that manner"

(Me)   "Sorry madam I haven't got time, I have other customers waiting, now do I repair your washing machine or do I go, the choice madam is yours"?

(Customer) "I will not allow you anywhere near my machine, I will insist that you do not come here next time, now get orf my property". With that I left and because of the one less job I was able to finish on time for once. The next morning back in the yard my Boss asked to see me, I went in, he told me that the customer in Rufford had complained saying that I was rude and abusive. I told him the story and he was ok. He did say that with some customers you have to bite your tongue and not enter into any kind of debate. He did however find it very funny.

Wages in the domestic appliance game were very low even for the eighties, I would start work at 8am and get 8-10 calls and you had to finish them that was to prevent skiving off etc. bringing home £115 per week. Most days in my early years I would not be getting home until well after 7pm, meaning, with travelling, I was out of the house most days over twelve hours. One engineer asked me if I was married, I told him I was, he then told me that I wouldn't be married for long as this domestic appliance game is a marriage wrecker. I can remember telling him that my marriage has just had a massive test over the last 2 years so I don't think being home late is going to compare somehow. This life was harder than at the pit in some ways. It did have its benefits though, I remember very vividly one incident in Nottinghamshire I was calling at a house that insisted on first call, and this meant I had to be there before 08:30am. I arrived at the house, a very large property with a garden that could fit colliery row and the pit itself and still not find it for a week it was massive. The lady answered the door.

(Me)   "Good Morning, Bosch"

(Customer) "Oh yes won't you come in" (I thought to myself was that question or an invitation). I went in and the entrance led into the rather large kitchen, the dishwasher was next to the sink, and I had to fit a new motor. The woman was in her night dress which was quite short, she was a stunner too but that was beside the point. I tilted the dishwasher back against the unit top and placing a tea towel between the appliance top and the worktop to prevent scratching. I had to lay down to start unbolting the motor which was situated underneath. Whilst I was doing this the customer asked me if I would like a cup of tea. I accepted, she then straddled over me to fill the kettle at the sink which startled me a little. I looked up and saw right up her nightdress, golly she may have been rich but she couldn't afford knickers, there it was winking at me. I was embarrassed to say the least. She must have known I could see it. It wasn't until getting back to the yard and telling the lads the tale that I discovered that she was well known for that and that was why she insisted on first call. Obviously I neglected to tell my wife about that incident.

This industry was ironic, I had spent several years working underground with men, now I am working on the surface dealing only with women, talk about opposite ends of the spectrum. This life was varied and interesting, meeting different people every day all different in so many ways to each other, some customers were a pleasure to be with, others were an absolute pain in the arse I can tell you.

The miners' strike did appear to be so far away from this world. Until that was until one day I was asked to work for the northern division and that was mainly Leeds, Bradford, Sheffield, and Barnsley. All the villages in between too. One particular day I turned up in the office to collect my work sheets, as normal I scanned the areas and the faults reported by the customer, this was so I could judge by the fault description what the repair was likely to be and more importantly how long it would take, then I would sort into am and pm calls. Today's jobs were no different to any other, the usual types of repairs, bearing replacement, blocked pumps and carbon brush replacement. One of the jobs in Barnsley was a suspected bearing which would take about three hours, but then the customer name said Mrs. A Scargill. I froze to the spot, I showed it to one the other engineers that was in the office who worked this area regularly. I asked him if that name could be the Arthur Scargill, he said that it could be Anne Scargill. My god, there is no way on earth I am going to that address. I went to the Manager and showed him the worksheet, I told him that I was an ex miner and I didn't want to go to that address. He told me that I didn't have a choice in the matter. I told him in no uncertain terms that I was not going to that address and that was final. He told me to sit down. I sat opposite him at his desk and he said.

(Boss) "Look what's the problem here Steve?"

(Me) "As you now know I'm an ex coal miner from the Derbyshire coal field"

(Boss) "Yes I know, you're among friends here, my son works at Woolley colliery in Barnsley. He was a staunch supporter of the strike in fact Arthur Scargill himself started work at Woolley"

(Me) "Well ok but what you don't know is that I was definitely not in favour of the strike and I went back to work during the strike". I was now holding my breath waiting to see how he would respond to that bombshell.

(Boss) "Bloody hell, you mean you are a scab"?

(Me) "No, I'm an engineer"

(Boss) "Engineer you might be, but god you scabbed"

(Me) "If that's the way you want to put it, then so be it"

(Boss) "Me and my brother who as you know runs the Southern division, come from a strong mining family we are the only two that don't work at the pit, moreover we used Dads money when he died to start this business as he was insistent that we didn't go down the pit, now I come to think about it Alan said to me he thought he saw you on TV when they ran the anniversary stuff"

(Me) "yes, that would have been me" I was by now feeling very uncomfortable, I found myself sat amidst a mining family whose son stayed out on strike, Jesus how did I end up here?

(Boss) "So what do we do now? Personally, I couldn't care less who or what you are but I do have a business to run and a business that has a lot of people associated with the pits and those that aren't sympathised with the miners, bloody hell aren't you in the wrong pace"?

(Me) "Well whatever, I appreciate you have a business to run, but I aint going to that address"

(Boss) "Well if you're worried about your safety your secret is safe with me, just go, and don't mention the strike and do the job and leave"

(Me) "No, you're not listening, I am not refusing because I'm worried, I'm refusing because I do not want to do anything for that guy, furthermore if he's there, there will be a problem, I will guarantee that"

(Boss) "Look at the end of the day, we're not even sure it is that Scargill, but in view of what you say, I will give it to one of the other lads but you will have to take two extra jobs off the engineer as it will be out of his area"

(Me) "That's not a problem but it would be easier to just swap altogether that way none of us are inconvenienced"

(Boss) "Oh, not satisfied with destroying the NUM you want to now want to tell me how to run my business"

(Me) "Tell you what, shove it! I aint tecking that from you or anyone else"

(Boss) "Look calm down Steve, go home today and I will see you in the Morning when we've both had time to think"

(Me)   "I don't need to think, I'm gone, I will go back to my own area in Nottingham, if there's still a problem then so be it".

With that I left but I was angry, I drove back home but I couldn't remember any of the journey, my mind was so full of what had just taken place. I was beginning to wonder whether I would come across this for the rest of my working life.

The following day I reported back to my normal office, my boss was in and I went in to see him, after discussing yesterday with him he was very understanding, he didn't share the same opinion of his brother and was happy for me to continue in the Southern region. I was somewhat relieved but still upset. My Boss told me that he didn't have the same sympathy for the miners that his brother did. His nephew did work at Woolley colliery as his brother had said but was supported financially from the business, so the strike was no hardship for him at least.

I was certain that the strike would actually follow me where ever I worked, but the effects would be varied and would also diminish as time went on.

It was at about this time when I got on one of my work sheets a call to Nottingham Forest football club, this was a bonus to me as I was a forest supporter, and the job was to install a gas tumble dryer near the changing rooms. It was here that I met Brian Clough, he was giving a pep talk to some of the players in the usual Brian Clough style. When I told him that I was a forest fan he couldn't have been any less bothered. Upon leaving he came back to me and threw me a white short sleeved shirt with the European champions badge on it, I was so delighted with this I still have it today.

On one particular day my van had a clutch problem and was deemed necessary to book it in for repair, so I had to double up with another engineer. The engineer was telling me how he was planning to leave and set up on his own, then he asked me if I would work for him. He said that he could match the wage and guarantee only local calls to Worksop, Mansfield and Retford area. This was appealing so I told him that I would wait six months to allow him to establish then I would come and work for him.

By the end of that year I had left and gone to work for him. Unfortunately he went under and I was made redundant just six months into my employment with him.

So it was 1987 and I was between jobs as it were, the next bombshell was in September that year, my dear Grandma had died, we had planned a holiday in Scotland with the wife's mum and dad. The funeral was planned for the Monday. My father in law offered to drive me back down from Scotland for the funeral, that was a very generous offer but I couldn't allow him to do that, the funeral would have been difficult enough but my mother and my dad and Uncle Tony would be there, that would have made the situation even harder. If I had not been in Scotland though I would have gone absolutely no question of that. I decided to pay my own respects to my Grandma as soon as I returned from Scotland.

CHAPTER 16

The next big challenge

In 1989 my father in law died, this obviously was tragic for both me and my wife, That man did more for me in the few short years that I had known him than my own father ever did in 21 years. His death hit us hard and I took it very hard too and was very upset for a few weeks after, it was like I had lost two dads in relatively quick succession. I just hope he knew how much I loved him and how grateful I was to him.

I knew that my wife was messing around and I also knew that now her dad had died she would find it easier to leave. Thankfully he wasn't aware of the difficulties we were having, or of her affairs. We soon separated and it would seem that this marriage is heading for the divorce courts. In a way I wasn't that surprised, she was quite popular in the village before the strike and within a very short time she had lost her job, her friends and was dragged into a war zone. She was young, we were both young but she was younger than I was and was a social girl, whereas I wasn't, I couldn't go out in the village pubs drinking even if I wanted to. There would always be trouble if I had done.

I divorced my wife and we were now moving on, my daughter was living with her mother and her latest. I was powerless to do anything, I knew at the bottom of my heart that my daughter would be better off with her mother but I did ask my solicitor about custody, the bleak truth was that I am unemployed and wouldn't be able to provide for her properly, and if I found a job I wouldn't be able to be there for her, it was a vicious circle. My wife was unfaithful to me but I couldn't fault her mothering skills.

Steve my best mate had separated from his wife for the same reasons as I had. We spent most of our new found spare time together, Steve took his separation very hard and was struggling to cope, I was not ecstatic at my situation but I was coping well, emotionally at least.

One particular day Steve came round to my house as normal, but he wasn't normal, he seemed spaced out somewhat. I asked him if he was ok, he said he was. He could barely keep his eyes open, then I noticed a silver foil pack in his hands that he was clutching. I asked him what it was, but he shrugged it off saying it was just pain killers. He said he needed some fresh air and was going to sit on the bench on hangar hill in the village, this was a popular spot and was just a hundred yards from my house. I told him I would come with him, but I just needed to nip next door and I would catch him up. When he left I went next door and asked her if I could use her phone, she agreed. I rang Steve's dad and told him that I suspected Steve had overdosed on pain killers, I told him where Steve was and he said he would be there in a few minutes. I rushed back up to Steve who was sat on the bench but barely conscious. After about 5 minutes his dad came and picked him up and rushed him off to Bassetlaw hospital. It later transpired that Steve was within twenty minutes of being unconscious and most probably would have died had he been alone. He recovered after a few days and was receiving the help that he needed. I made it my business to be extra vigilant with him, but eventually it seemed he was coping.

I soon found another job with a domestic appliance firm in Sheffield. The wage was extremely low and I worked out that after paying my mortgage now that the social security wasn't paying I was worse off by £5 per week. On the plus side I was getting out and about and meeting new people. And I had a vehicle for my own use, I knew that it was the only way to go as I was low on options.

The work here is lower class mostly and I was working on mainly Candy and Hoover appliances, which were all under guarantee work. They did have a contract with AEG which was a high class German manufacturer. One of my first calls that I remember vividly is a call I had to a candy washing machine on the Manor top in Sheffield. I pulled up outside the house, the house didn't look anything like what I was used to with Bosch. There was a little boy of about 5 years old playing in the mud in the garden, he immediately jumped up and ran to the front door which was open and shouted "Mam, fucking wesher man's ere". Oh my god what have I come to here? I knocked on the door, and the event went something as follows.

(Me)   knock.....knock.....knock
(Customer) "Yeah"
(Me)   "Good morning, it's Candy"
(Customer) "Yea ok, bring thee sen in"

I walked in wiping my feet on the door mat, soon realising that I would be better off wiping my feet on the way out. The customer told me that there was a grating noise coming from the drum. I told her that it was probably a bra wire and it would take about 2 hours to remove as it involved taking the drum out. I also told her that although the appliance was under warranty, a bra wire is not covered as that is not the fault of the manufacturer.

(Customer) "How the fuck did a bra wire get in there I don't have bras
               with wires in"? (She lifted her scruffy moth eaten top up
               to show me her bra). "Look, no wires in them"
(Me)   "Well it sounds very much like a bra wire to me, but I will
               take off the pump hose and see if I can get a look"
I pulled out the machine and took off the hose, sure enough I could
               see it wrapped round the heating element.
(Me)   "Yes it's definitely a bra wire"
(Customer) "so how much is that gonna cost"?
(Me)   "It's about £90 including VAT"
(Customer) "I can't afford that, Couldn't you make something up so
               that it's covered under the guarantee"?
This put me in a quandary, I have never been asked that before, but it
               was clear by the surroundings that she couldn't afford that.
(Me)   "Right, I will see if I can get it from the heater socket,
               it's a long shot but it has been done, it will destroy the
               heater in the process and I can replace the heater under
               the guarantee. The fault description you gave to the office

was a grating noise, which can happen with heater fault
as they can curl upwards catching the drum"

(Customer) "Thank you I do appreciate that, and I can make it worth
your while for doing it"

(Me) "That's ok, I don't mind really, but you don't have to pay
me anything, really it's no problem"

(Customer) "Oh right, I wasn't offering money cos I'm skint"

I looked at her rather embarrassed, thinking that the quicker I get this job done the better. Even though I was single, it was a big no no with the Company as with all service companies, but I had known it happen. But she was bloody filthy, the house was filthy, obviously her mind was filthy and I wasn't desperate, well, not that desperate anyway. I started repairing the machine and she asked me if I wanted a cuppa. Not wishing to offend, after all I had just turned down whatever else she was wanting to give me, so I accepted. When the tea came it came in a cup that looked like she had been using it as a toilet. I tipped the tea in the washing machine when her back was turned. I finished the repair and made a hasty getaway.

At the office there was another engineer that I befriended, he lived on the outskirts of Sheffield to the south, and was only about fifteen minutes from Whitwell. On the occasions that his van was off the road I was able to pick him up and vice versa. One morning I had to pick him up I called round to his house, I was invited in as he wasn't quite ready, his wife was pleasant but a little strange. She was a vegetarian and a traditionalist, not liking the modern appliances of the day and still used the old irons that had to be heated up on the fire. She came across as being quite forward and was very flirty, it was obvious to me that this was to make her husband jealous, like I said weird. He had often told me that the relationship could be volatile at times and she did like coming on to people to make him jealous. One morning when I called to pick him up I was invited in as normal, when I sat down she started having a go at me, she was complaining that I had left Kitkat wrappers in his van on one of the occasions I had used his van, I looked at my mate and he was gesturing to me as if to say to go along with it. I did do that and said I couldn't remember it but I would make sure next time that I wouldn't leave them in there. When we set off to the office he told me that she was against him eating chocolate as some companies tested their products on animals. He had a Kitkat and forgot to discard the wrapper so he blamed it on me to get himself out of trouble.

Another emotive experience was on a call out in Hathersage in Derbyshire, I had been called to a candy washing machine that had a noise issue. Upon examining the machine I noticed that the inner drum was dented beyond belief, it was obvious that she had put something in there that it wasn't designed for. I put this to her and she broke down in tears telling me that her husband had put bricks in it before putting it on a spin cycle, she went on to say how she found a note in one of his pockets from another woman, it was obvious from the note that he had been having extramarital relations. When she confronted him with this they had a massive row and she went to her Mothers for the night. When she came back in the morning he had destroyed half the house and packed his stuff and gone, they had been together for over 20 years. I was now in uncharted territory for me and I wasn't comfortable being faced with a woman who was in quite some distress. I told her not to worry and I said jokingly the machine I can fix, the marriage was another matter. She laughed as she began to calm down, I told her that I could fit another inner drum as I had one in the van. She told me how her estranged husband had left her with practically nothing and that she would have to borrow the money to pay for the repair as she knew it wouldn't be covered by the guarantee. I told her that I would do it under guarantee and it wasn't a problem. The truth is I felt bit sorry for her and I did sympathise with the situation she was in. She asked me how long the job would take and I told her it would take a couple of hours. She looked at the clock and said "but that means it will be 7pm before you finish, what will your wife say"

(Me)   "I'm not married I am divorced"
(Customer) "Would you be offended then if I cooked some tea for you"?
(Me)   "No that would be nice". I was now thinking that this is an unusual situation to be in and my boss would not be impressed, but it was my last job of the day, after that it's my own time so not really a problem.
(Customer) "I was thinking of doing fish and chips, home cooked chips too"

(Me)   "Lovely that would be nice"

(Customer) "I am going to get a shower and changed, if you need to go out to your van for anything could you lock the door when you come back in"?

(Me)   "Yes no problem". The house was in the middle of nowhere in its own grounds so that request was not unusual. I started to strip down the machine to replace the drum, I was a little bothered that I was not going to get home until about 10pm but then at least I would not have to bother about cooking any tea. I was acutely aware that I was in a dangerous position too. I was accepting an offer of dinner from a vulnerable woman in a house in the middle of nowhere, I was leaving myself wide open to all sorts of allegations. I did however feel sorry for her situation and she did come across as quite savvy in a lot of ways.

She came down from the shower about half an hour later and I was shocked to see she had changed into her night wear. She must have noticed that I was a little alarmed and she told me not to worry as she always showered and changed at this time. She told me that she was usually in bed about eight. So I continued the repair and finished it in about two hours. Whilst the machine was on test she asked me if I would like to go into the dining room for the fish and chips that she had cooked. I told her that I was in my work clothes and that I didn't want to get oil anywhere. She said "that's alright we can eat in the kitchen diner then"

We started to eat the dinner and sure enough she was going on about her estranged husband, it was clear that she was hurt and angry. She asked me how I come to be on my own. I told her that I married too young but didn't go into details. I noticed that her clothing was loose and I could easily see her boobs and I think it was intentional. Despite all the bravado of other engineer's when they tell stories of being in this position I was actually quite scared. She was attractive, but vulnerable, she was not in complete control of her emotions that made for a very dangerous situation. I was keen to make an exit and soon started making motions towards wrapping up my tools. Surprisingly she was ok, and it wasn't until I asked her to sign the worksheet that she wrote on a piece of paper her number. She told me that if I was ever passing and wanted a cuppa to just ring and

I could call in. I agreed, thanked her for her hospitality and left, bloody sharpish at that.

On my way home I can remember thinking that maybe I should have hung around a bit because to be honest I was in with a chance and with a good looking woman too. But I knew I was only thinking that way because I was safe now.

Back at the office my close friend told me that he was leaving to take up a post with a major appliance firm in Castleford West Yorkshire. This was a bombshell to me as he was the only engineer I had really bonded with. I was friendly with some of the others but the Company I was with had a very high turnover of staff due to the very low wages and the curmudgeonly boss. That was not the reason he was leaving though, it was because he wanted to work on a national level for a national company. He told me that he would try and get me a job there once he had settled in.

I had another friend in the village who was an ex miner and worked at Welbeck colliery, Welbeck colliery was in Nottinghamshire and worked all the way through the strike. He was a very close friend and had a knack of telling you exactly the way it was whether it pleased or offended you. Since my marriage failed I spent quite a lot of time with him. Although very happily married one of his pastimes was to occasionally go to Roxy's night club in Sheffield. He persuaded me to tag along with him, so on Thursday nights I would get dressed up and toddle along with him, He always used to say that he was going to get me fixed up with a woman. We sat at the bar people watching for hours before leaving for home, I was getting back home at about 3:00am then getting up for work at 6:30am, looking back now I don't know how I managed that even though I was still young. It was here that I had a few dates with one of them becoming my second wife. She was 10 years older than me and we were not really compatible but struggled along for seven years, and it was a struggle. She had been married four times before and was very distrusting of men, she was always suspicious when I was out either on my own or later coming home than expected. This caused a lot of problems, as with my first marriage I was always faithful which tended to fuel resentment on my part of constantly being accused of infidelity, she always used to say that all the others had run off with younger women, it was only a matter of time before I did too. She couldn't see that it may have been her distrust and acting accordingly that drove her previous husbands away. Eventually this marriage failed too

CHAPTER 17

Life as a Domestic Appliance Engineer

I carried on doing the usual routine without anything out of the ordinary happening until one particular day I was asked to go to a call to a washing machine in Hathersage, this wasn't unusual in itself but the customer had requested that the office sent me. I asked the girl booking the calls why she had requested me, she said the lady said you called a few weeks ago and stayed very late to repair the machine and that you were a pleasure to have in her house. The address and customer name looked familiar but I couldn't quite pinpoint from where. When I arrived at the address I realised straight away that it was the woman who gave me fish and chips whose husband had left her. I made it my first call as I was in Chesterfield and Worksop in the afternoon. I walked down the driveway to the front door and knocked. The woman opened the door. She was not dressed but had a large towel wrapped around her body and a smaller one round her head.

(Customer) "Hello Steve, come on in". I followed her in, the fault sheet said that it was leaking, I noticed that the washing machine was in use.

(Me) "You say it's leaking"

(Customer) "Yes, I noticed yesterday that there was a small pool of water at the front of the machine, but nothing today so far".

(Me)	"Ok, I will just watch it for a minute then check it over for you"
(Customer)	"Alright Steve, I will put the kettle on. You must think me a right one, I always seem to be undressed when you come".
(Me)	"yeah, true, but it's the time of day that I come, last time being evening and now it's barely 8:30"
(Customer)	"I will just be through the hallway if you need me".
(Me)	"Ok, no worries".

I knelt down in front of the machine and started checking for leaks, there were no signs of leaks and no sign of it ever having leaked. Still I knelt there and just watched, it's possible it could be on rinse where it leaked and that would be clear water, the timer showed about 15 minutes from the rinse stages.

The customer came through with the tea, she told me she would put it on my tool case which was laid on the floor, as she bent over to put the cup down I glanced across, she still had towel robing on but I could see right up, plain as day no bloody knickers on. I quickly turned back away hoping she didn't see me look. She went back down the hallway without saying anything. At this point her phone rang which was in the hallway. I could tell it wasn't a pleasant call by her raised voice, she came back in to the kitchen and pulled the door to, which was good as it was a little embarrassing for her.

I was by now thinking that this call was just made up, the evidence seemed overwhelming, no fault with the machine yet, making reference to being undressed, bending down so I could see everything she had and more besides. Hmmm, I can't waste time too much time here. No sooner I had I thought that and there was a very small pool of water in front of the machine. I was now going to be here for another half an hour or so. I discovered that the door seal had a small hole in it which was just above the normal water level and would only be noticed during the rinse cycle when the water level was slightly higher. I didn't have a seal on the van for this model machine as I used it the day before. I went to the van and radioed another engineer that was working the same area but on AEG machines, he confirmed he had a seal on his van and I arranged to meet him nearby to pick it up. I went back into the house and I could still hear her yelling on the phone. I wrote a note on some paper on the table telling her that I was just nipping out to get a door seal and would be back in about twenty minutes.

I picked up the seal and went back to the house. I knocked and waited a couple of minutes, when there was no answer I just knocked and walked in but calling Hello as I went in. The door entered directly into the kitchen so I opened the door to the machine and looked for somewhere to put the wet washing. There was nowhere obvious so I went to find the customer. I opened the hallway door and called "Hello". I continued walking down the hallway and she was sat in the dining room still in her bath robes but crying her eyes out. She looked at me then wiped her eyes and said "I'm sorry about that I'm just a bit upset"

(Me)   "That's alright, it can't be easy, I was just wondering where to put the washing out of the machine"

(Customer) "Oh, I see, er I will get a bowl and come and get it for you".

I went back into the kitchen and started to pull the machine out so I could remove the lid. The customer came through with a laundry bowl.

(Customer) "I'm sorry about that Steve, it's just that my husband is telling me he can't pay the mortgage here and on his fancy woman's place too, bloody men they should be shot at birth every one of them, there all bastards".

She started crying again, bloody hell, what do I do here.

(Me)   "Would you like me to come back some other time to repair the machine? I can see that it's not a good time".

She walked over to me and put her hand on my shoulder and said. "No, I didn't mean what I said about all men, I would be happy if you could stay and fix the machine now, I'm just so angry at the minute"

(Me)   "Ok I will carry on and it will only take about thirty minutes".

(Customer) "Can I ask you a question? And give me truthful answer"

(Me)   "Yes no worries". I was dreading what was coming next, she was not in a stable condition at all.

(Customer) "As a man, do you find me attractive?"

Jesus H Christ there's no right answer to that. She was attractive and I think she knew it, but if I confirm it what will her reaction be, if I lie and say no, she will be offended and who knows what will happen then?

(Me)   "Of course you are attractive, anyone can see that".

(Customer) "Then why does he say I'm an old worn out prune that no one would touch with a barge pole"?

(Me)   "I don't really think, he means it, he's obviously trying to hurt you, he wouldn't have married you if he thought that".

(Customer) "Aww thanks for that, you have really cheered me up, would you like a cuppa, looks like that one is cold"?

(Me)   "Yes please, that would be nice".

She went back through the hallway, I breathed a sigh of relief, I wasn't at all sure how that was going to end.

I continued the repair, then I heard her shout. "Steve, would you mind giving me a hand for one minute"?

(Me)   "Yes, no problem".

I walked through towards the dining room, (customer) "in here".

I pushed open a door on my left where the voice came from, it was rather large bedroom, she was at the far end with a big cardboard box on the ottoman at the foot of the bed. I walked towards her and the box. (Customer) "I just need to move this box onto the floor".

(Me)   "Ah, ok". I put my hands in the handle inserts and lifted the box, blimey it was heavy. I lowered it to the floor, before I could stand up I saw the towelling robe crumple on the floor in front of the box. I turned round and stood up facing the other way so as not to see what was obviously going to be her naked. She got hold of my right hand and pulled me round, I knew now there was no doubt what she wanted, the penny had dropped and clanging like a dustbin lid. As she pulled me round I saw her in all her glory, for a woman in her 40's she looked well. She looked at me smiling.

(Customer) "Don't look so scared, you said you fancied me didn't you"?

(Me) "er, well, not exactly, I said you were attractive, not quite the same".

(Customer) "So you don't fancy me then"?

(Me) "I didn't say that either, but this is not right, I could get sacked".

(Customer) "well I certainly don't intend telling your boss, you are single, I am separated, nobody is going to get hurt, I just want to be loved at the moment, I'm not offering marriage, I just want you to make love to me, what's wrong with that"?

(Me) "It's not that I don't want to, and it's not that I don't fancy you, it's just not right, you could feel differently later then I could be in all sorts of trouble".

(Customer) "Are you scared of me, do I frighten you"?

(Me) "I'm scared of the situation, you don't realise the predicament you have put me in, in a different situation at a different time I would jump at it, but now is not the right time".

She got my hand and placed it on her breast, I pulled it away, and I was bloody petrified.

(Customer) "Ok not to worry, I feel bloody stupid and embarrassed now, I'm sorry, of course you are probably right".

She picked up the towel and wrapped it back around her.

I went back into the kitchen to finish off the machine. I then packed my tools back up. She came into the kitchen and was fully dressed. I gave her the worksheet for her to sign. She signed it and asked me if I was ok, and had she offended me.

I told her I was ok and that I wasn't offended, far from it, I also told her that she should not blame herself for the actions of others and that any man would think her attractive, I said she was a stunner and had a figure to match and that marriages can go stale, I knew that only too well, men and women for that matter can always think that the grass is greener elsewhere. She told me that I was a rare gentleman and that most men would have taken advantage of the situation, she told me that, she really did like not only my attitude but my manner and if I changed my mind then to ring her and we could try again in a more comfortable setting. I told her I would. I left the house knowing full well that I wouldn't.

I told one of the other engineers, he found it amusing and told me I was mad not taking her to bed and giving her one as he put it. I still think even to this day that if I had of, I would have regretted it, but god I was bloody tempted, very tempted. But she only had to come to her senses afterwards and scream rape to the police and my life would have been ruined. I can just see all you guys thinking. That given that situation a good looking woman stark bollock naked asking to be bedded you wouldn't need asking twice, it's the stuff that dreams are made of right! The reality is guys that yes I would have thought exactly the same, but when you are in that situation you will think very differently, take my word for it.

This situation is exactly why service companies do not like customers requesting engineer's by name. The situation I just described is a hazard of the job along with speeding tickets and parking tickets. Another hazard of the job is dogs. I remember visiting a customer in Rotherham, an area that was rough to say the least. I walked down the path and knocked on the door, a girl opened the letter box and told me to go round the back because of the dog. I opened the gate that had lots of beware of the dog signs with pictures of a Doberman dog. I went through and started to walk down the side of the house towards the rear of the house. As I did so the Doberman came round the corner and had met me half way, it was slavering from its mouth and was picking up speed and snarling, I knew it was going to attack me. It launched itself at me and I raised my right foot to kick it in the mouth, the dog caught me by my foot and dragged me to the ground, shaking it's head and snarling with my foot in his teeth, I managed to open my clip on my tool box and the first that fell out was my bull nose hammer, it's now going to be a Doberman nose hammer. I slammed the hammer straight down onto the head of the dog, it yelped and went to one side and laid on the grass, it looked as though I had killed it but I only stunned it, my foot now with only half a shoe on it was bleeding quite badly. After a brief argument with the customer I managed to drive myself to Rotherham hospital for treatment, the Triage nurse temporarily dressed the wound then told me I had to go to my own hospital for proper treatment and tetanus injection. I then had to drive to Bassetlaw hospital to be treated properly. Whilst I was waiting in the waiting room there was a postman nearby with a bandage round his leg. He looked at me and asked if it was a dog, I told him that it was, he then told me his was too and that his boss would write a letter to the owner telling them that if it happened again they would have to collect their post from the local office. I found it funny however when the postman said that, the irony there was he would be the one who would have to deliver the letter.

Talking about irony, one day I was sat at home watching the formula 1 grand prix when there was a knock at my front door, I answered the door and there stood a guy who had been very active on the picket lines in the miners' strike. He asked me if I would look at his washer for him. I was staggered, although the strike was now well behind us feelings were still very much running high. I agreed to do it and told him I would be round after the grand prix. So after the grand prix I got in the van and drove round to his house. I knocked on the door.

(Miner) "Hi Stevie lad bring thi sen in me old cock". I went in but still finding the situation strange and not that comfortable.

(Miner) "Aar lass reckons it aint spinning and when she bangs the machine it starts spinning and blue sparks are cumin art from underneath"

(Me) "Yeah that'll be carbon brushes"

(Miner) "Arr much is that gunna cost mi"?

(Me) "Well I can get some from a supplier who supplies to trade in Worksop, be about a tenner"

(Miner) "a fuckin tenner, is that all"? The reasoning behind me only charging cost with a little bit extra was to try to make him feel bad about the grief he had dished out on the picket line.

I actually had the spare in my shed, so I went back and got them, then returned to fit them. Whilst I was fitting them he said "is thi faather talking to thi yet young un"?

(Me)   "No,"
(Miner)   "Well its abart time the daft cunt got ovver it, fuck sake its ovver and done WI nar"
(Me)   "yeah but he's a stubborn old goat, he will never come round I don't think"
(Miner)   "That's fuckin stupid, my nephew went fuckin back after 3 months, am rate enough wi im nar"
(Me)   "That's how it should be". I completed the job, he gave me £20 and I left. That was totally unexpected but a good sign.

He wasn't the only one though, I specifically remember a guy stopping me in the co-op, and he asked me if I knew anything about TV, not sure if he was looking for an argument or he was for real,
I said "yes there square boxes with moving pictures on them"
He said "very fuckin funny, but dus tha know how to fix um"?

(Me)   "Depends what the problem is I know a little bit but not enough to say I can fix um tho".
(Miner)   not to worry, I understand where tha coming from, if I wah thee I wunt fix it either"
(Me)   "No, don't get me wrong, if I knew what the problem was I would do it". "What's up wi it"?
(Miner)   "It's a push button channel thingy that waint stay in".
(Me)   "Ok I might be able to fix that, is it a Fergusson be any chance?"
(Miner)   "kinell arr the fuck did tha know that"? (Me)   "There prone to it and I have a new channel selector for one of them in me shed, I'll pop round about 6ish if you like".
(Miner)   "Can a be cheeky and ask thee to come before, cos crickets on BBC 2 at 6".
(Me)   "Ok see thee abart fooer then".

I went round at four and he was in the garden levelling out some gravel. He looked up and saw me then said "eyup marra, arr lass reckoned you wunt show up".

(Me)   "Arr well not to worry".

We went inside and I soon fitted the new channel selector, the old one was wedged in with a match stick, he asked me how much I owed him, again I only charged a tenner, truth is the part cost more than that but there were very few of them old fergies around now, the likelihood of me needing it in the future was quite remote.

To be fair to the guy, he was a little embarrassed at his behaviour but I doubt whether he would have spoken had he not needed something from me.

CHAPTER 18

Ten Years on

It was now March 1994, it was fast approaching the 10th anniversary of the strike, ten years it seemed as though it was only yesterday. I went into the office as normal and my boss said he wanted to see me in his office. I followed up the very steep stairs to his office. That the office had received a telephone call from a national newspaper and Yorkshire television wanting to speak to me. He asked me why they would want to speak to me and wondered whether it was something that would affect him and his business. The conversation went something like as follows.

(Me)   "ah yes, I think I know what that's all about"

(Boss) "I don't want to pry or interfere in your private life, but I regard you as a good engineer and popular with my customers, so if you are in any trouble I might be able to help you"

(Me)   "I'm not in any trouble as such, it's just that in a former life I was a coal miner as you know, I broke the strike and returned to work six months into it. The newspapers and TV news took a great interest in my story because my dad was on strike throughout and disowned me because I went back"

(Boss) "Oh, I see, I didn't know about that, I saw all that stuff on the news at the time but didn't really take a great deal of notice as it didn't affect me too much, I had no connections with the mining industry. For what it's worth I think Scargill was a communistic dictator whose only desire was to bring down the conservative government, as for your dad, it's his loss, I can't imagine what the whole experience was like for you, I don't think I would have the guts to cross an angry picket line no matter what my principles were. I admire you for that. I was beginning to think you were in serious trouble, it's not every day that you have the newspapers and TV chasing you. It's that if it was something very serious and you were a mass murderer or something then I wouldn't have wanted my company being associated with you, I hope you understand what I mean"?

(Me)   "Yes, I know what you mean, this is just something I have to deal with now and again and because it's the tenth anniversary, and my dad still doesn't want to know me, it makes for topical news".

With that now he knew his company's image wasn't going to be tarnished he was fine, he never mentioned it again or asked how things were with regard to me and my dad.

When I arrived home that evening, my neighbour came round, she told me that there has been a lot of activity around my house with reporters and TV crews asking where I was. She told them that she thought I was working away. I remember telling her that nobody is able to evade the British media, they are experts at finding people. So does this mean now that I am going to be chased down at every anniversary of the strike? Will my life not be my own? Still I was certain that I wouldn't be doing any interviews with ITV again after the last episode, they can't be trusted.

I went to the paper shop as normal and the owner said that the news of the world newspaper had been in there asking questions about me. He said he told them to bugger off. I was thankful for that, I know their style of reporting and they would only be interested in blowing the family situation out of all proportion.

There was a lot of coverage on the news about the 10th anniversary but there was no mention of me and there was no interviews with my dad. The more he kept quiet the more I knew he was inwardly ashamed of his behaviour, if he wasn't then he should be. I had a lot of hurt and anger with regards to my dad, but the TV is not the stage to slug it out. I had every intention of doing this one to one and man to man someday.

I was however contacted by a popular TV show on Channel 4, they wanted to discuss the family situation, a bit like Jeremy Kyle show, but obviously it wasn't for that show. They said they would have my mum and dad and my brother on the show to help sort the problem out. I told them that I would not air my problems out on TV just for the entertainment of others, its real life to me I am the one living it every day. The truth of the matter was that I didn't think my dad would ever go on TV and battle against me or anyone else for that matter, but the overriding reason I wouldn't take part was that if my mother was on there trying to come across the innocent party stuck in the middle then I would be forced into confronting her over the abuse I suffered at her evil hands from birth. I was confident that neither of them would be as stupid as to agree to it, however I told the researcher that if they agreed then I would have no option but to agree to it also. My brother told them he would not be appearing on the show. My dad obviously refused because they never got back to me, but I did tape all the shows for a while just in case it was done without me.

In March 1995 the tenth anniversary since the end of the strike was upon us, with the same usual rhetoric on TV and in the newspapers.

I was contacted by another chat show for ITV wanting to do an update, I refused point blank. They told me that it was in the public interest that I told my story and that the journalism that was in place in 1985 is not the same that is in place today, however my answer remained the same.

A few weeks after this, I was contacted by a major electrical goods retailer to see if I would work for them as an engineer in their white goods workshop. I arranged to go for an interview at their distribution centre in Castleford, West Yorkshire on the coming Saturday. The guy who was to interview me was the service Manager. He gave me a written technical test to complete. He marked that from the answer sheet he had, then conducted the interview. He told me about the Company and that the workshop that I was working in was next to the main warehouse which employed about 300 warehouse operatives. The comment that stopped me dead was when he said that they were mostly former Yorkshire miners. I had to tell him about my past and that I worked during the miners' strike. He realised straight away the issues with this, then he went on to say that he wasn't about to tell anyone and he was dam sure I wouldn't. He said that it would be best if we kept it secret. He also said that he could not guarantee that it would never leak out and that if it did I may have to leave for my own safety. I wasn't sure at this moment whether taking this job was the right thing to do. I told him that I would like to digest all that and could I mull it over for a while. He was very accommodating and agreed to give me a week before needing a decision.

I thought about it over the weekend. This was a difficult decision but surprisingly I made the decision really quickly. When I got into work on Monday I handed in my notice. My boss took this very badly and we ended up falling out over it, which made the decision all the easier.

I rang the service manager and told him that I had handed my notice in and would like to accept his offer. I arranged to start for the following Monday and I was to be picked up by one of his engineers who lived locally to Whitwell.

I started work as planned and was given the guided tour of the distribution centre, it was a massive building and there was people buzzing round everywhere, not to mention fork lift trucks. In the white goods workshop there was only the two of us to deal with all the returns nationwide from their stores, sometimes in excess of 40 appliances per day. Later that week my colleague said that he usually takes his lunchtime in the warehouse workers cabin, so I agreed to do that with him. They were a great bunch of lads to be honest and I fitted in very well. It was never long before their topic of conversation got round to the miners' strike, I refrained from getting involved as they weren't aware that I had worked at the pit too. I had a laugh one day when I was sat in there, there was about 30 of them in the room when the guy sat next to me pipes up and says" I could smell a scab a fuckin mile away" My colleague gave me a little sideways glance, as he was well aware. When we got back to our workshop we had a good laugh about that comment. The warehouse lads were full of stories about their flying picket days and the battles they had with the police. Despite the seriousness of the situation I was always comfortable around them, so long as they didn't twig on I was safe.

The service Manager was quite a character and as bosses go him was easy going, he had days when he would be firm but he was always fair.

About a year after working there, my colleague took a job with Zanussi as a field service engineer, which left me alone in the workshop. I was able to secure the Company van for use to commute to and from work, I also did customer and branch visits. I became very popular with some of the warehouse lads and spent some time with them, I often used to think to myself that if someone had ever said to me around the time of the strike that I would be working amidst 300 Yorkshire Miner's I would have thought they were in cloud cuckoo land. Life can be very strange at times. One thing that was abundantly clear is that they were just as bitter about the tory government and the strike breakers now as they were back then.

Upstairs on the first floor was the call centre and brown goods workshop, I got very friendly with one of the brown goods engineer's, Kenny, I was friendly with all of them but Ken and me hit it off extremely well, so well that I let him in on my secret. My trust in Ken was well placed and we are still very good friends to this day. Ken was the senior brown goods engineer and he covered the white goods workshop when I was on holiday or off sick. Ken is multi-talented and a very good and loyal friend and colleague, He was the type of guy that would give you his last penny. Ken lived in Sheffield and was not associated directly with the coal mining Industry.

Occasionally I would go to lunch with the store keeper, he was a natural comic and was very popular with everybody, one particular hot summer's day he asked me if I wanted to go to lunch in nearby Pontefract town centre, I was sceptic at first because we only had half an hour for lunch and the trip alone was 10 minutes' drive. Despite this we went and we decided to go into a pub for a snack, he was a good beer drinker unlike me and had a good few beers. Time passed us by and it was soon nearly two hours past, which meant we had gone over our half hour lunch break by an hour and a half. We headed back to work and hoped that we hadn't been missed, but the service Manager had been ringing my workshop for me and had gone down to the workshop to find me. I had not long got back in the workshop when he rang down again and told me to go up to his office. I went up there and the store keeper was already in his office, he asked us where we had been, we didn't see any point in lying so we told him. He went ballistic and really tore strips off us, at the end he went on to say that the thing that pissed him off the most was that we hadn't invited him. That was the type of guy he was, he could have made a really big deal over that but didn't. He knew that anyone who worked for him would go the extra mile for him without question.

Before long a new management team came in who worked previously with a major rival, this is when life changed for everyone, the new management managed with a deep resentment of existing staff, my service manager was the major butt of all the cynicism and vindictive attitudes from the new management. I often found myself being protective of the service Manager and challenged the new management at every opportunity, the service Manger was professional as ever, despite being openly victimised in front of his former staff. This treatment was horrific to watch and witness and it was a very major cause of the service Manager's major breakdown and in my personal opinion a contributing factor of his illnesses that led to his cancer. I know this sounds very harsh, but I witnessed this brutal treatment and stand by my accusations, I too became a victim of their cruel nature.

The Company were being taken over by another major appliance retailer and as a result led to widespread redundancies. It was announced by the current management that anyone at risk,(which was all of us) would be looked at favourably for being paid off should they find work before being given a date to leave. I went to my immediate manager who confirmed that as I was the only white goods engineer and as the new company were making some of their white goods engineer redundant, then I would be made redundant in the next 90 days. I secured a new position with another company and was told they must insist I started within 4 weeks as per my notice requirements, I was pressured heavily to start sooner than that or the offer of employment would be revoked.

I then went back to my manager and reminded him of the statement that they would look favourably. They said that they were waiting for my confirmed leaving date which by the way had changed twice already, they told me with a glint of satisfaction that if I accepted the new job then I will have resigned. My new employer insisted I started as soon as possible and would not wait for a confirmed leaving date that may change time and time again.

My opinion was that it is better to be in full time work than be sat in the dole with £8000 in my pocket. Needless to say I left but I have resented Company and everything about them ever since. Company of old would not have treated its employees that way.

(Nb. If anyone whom I have referred to here is reading this and challenges the comments, I would be only too happy to take this up with them, just as I have done since leaving in 2005).

CHAPTER 19

Changing Direction

I left the Company very bitter at being duped out of my redundancy payment. I was now starting work for my new Company at their Leeds factory. The Company was set up by the Government in 1945 primarily to provide employment and support to servicemen disabled during the war. It has grown with the times but has long since stopped being primarily for ex-servicemen and the like. Its mission is to provide sustainable work to disabled people and people who have significant barriers to work. Ethically this is a good service but I was astonished to find that it was one of the governments biggest secrets, not many people have actually heard of The Company and those that had known little of what it is about.

I was employed as a service engineer which was a team leading role, my remit was to train disabled people to repair and service domestic appliances. Appliances were sourced from civic amenity sites and then brought back to serviceability in the workshop. I initially complained to management that working on appliances from the dump and turning them back into the community was fraught with issues, Customer safety is paramount and at that moment in time I was the only person in The Company who had received correct manufacturer training. Management said that the Government wanted to reduce waste going to landfill by reuse and recycling. This meant that I was responsible for training, safety, and quality of product. A large task and on top of that I was working with people with varying disabilities. This was going to be a challenge, the only thing the disabled people didn't lack was will power and determination. They were a great bunch of people, I was apprehensive at first as I had never integrated with disabled people before, this wasn't through choice but merely that I had previously been involved in careers that would have been difficult for people with disabilities. Nonetheless I took on the challenge my greatest challenge was not being aware of the laws pertaining to disabled people and I would have to be careful not to say anything that would be offensive to them, obviously not through choice but through ignorance.

The work was totally alien to what I was used to, I even saw appliances coming into the workshop that I had condemned whilst working in my last job. They were banged and crumpled in places with bits missing. This is not going to be easy, but my guys were willing and compliant and a great bunch of young men and women. We were all learning. I was learning about them and their disabilities and what their capabilities were. The biggest barrier disabled people were facing was the attitudes and I could see that ignorance was a barrier to able bodied people. I realised that there but for the grace of god go I, any one of us could quite easily end up being in the same position as these guys through no fault of our own, disabilities from learning difficulties, physical disabilities through to heart attack victims etc. The list is endless, I admired each and every one of them and soon became not just their team leader but their friend. Management were mainly interested in balance sheets, but the management at factory level in most cases were appreciative and sympathetic to the employee's challenges in life. I learned quickly, I had to. There was a strong union presence within the organisation with members of the UNITE and GMB unions working in the factory. I was soon asked if I would join the GMB union by the GMB shop steward, I did so and was amazed when they said they would try to fight and retrieve my redundancy money that I missed out on in my last job. Hey, this is good at last, a union that actually believes in its members and not its own political interests. The action failed, primarily due to the looking favourably comment being verbal rather than in writing, I was infuriated because local management intimated that it would be paid, but hey, that's done with now, time to move on and put that behind me well for now at least.

Pretty soon the workshop was in full swing and the employees were trained to a decent standard, The Company decided to publicise its operation and invite VIP's to open the facility formally. This resulted in David Bellamy OBE and their Royal highnesses, Prince Edward and the Countess of Wessex. I soon found myself explaining the principles of refrigeration and how it is used in fridge freezers to David Bellamy, he was a gentleman and was also interested, he was keen to know more about the new refrigerant that was ozone friendly which was to replace the dangerous R12 refrigerant which turned to mustard gas when exposed to a naked flame. He knew all about its properties and as an environmental campaigner was very knowledgeable in the field, thank god I didn't bullshit him. Next was His Royal Highness Prince Edward and the Countess of Wessex. They were delightful if not a little ignorant as to what some of the appliances were. I did a full introduction to my team and they were charming, and my team were pleased for their visit. So I can remember that not all that long ago I was that snotty nosed scruffy kid on Colliery row, and now I was shaking hands with celebrities and royalty. I was proud, not too sure my dad would have been, considering he openly campaigns for the abolishment of royalty, and here was his son not only crossing picket lines but hob knobbing with royalty. It's a great shame that I won't be able to tell him. Ok that was a cynical comment, but funny nonetheless. Maybe the move to this company was a good one and perhaps things could improve from here on in.

I was living in a flat in Chesterfield after my separation from my second wife. I soon found myself being tired of going back to an empty flat. With nothing but my own company, don't get me wrong I do enjoy my own company but I do hanker after the happiness that most people enjoy. I had made two mistakes already on this front but didn't fall into the trap of thinking that all women were the same. I decided to join an online dating agency but not a free one, I decided I was going to join a subscription one with the hope of meeting a woman who was serious in finding love and happiness rather than a one night fling. I did have a casual relationship with a woman in Chesterfield but this was never going to be happy ever after both of us knew that, shamefully I have to admit here that maybe I did use her to some degree but I never led her on. It served mutual benefit at the time. I had subscribed to a dating agency online Udate and within a couple of days met Debbie, She looked and sounded wonderful and lived in Grantham in Lincolnshire. It was Saturday and I arranged to meet her in Grantham on the Monday night,

I knew this was going to be hard, driving from Leeds to Chesterfield after work then shower and change then on to Grantham, but I never did anything that was easy. So I drove over to her address where she was ready and waiting, I also noticed that she had two beautiful cats, Lulu and Midget, gorgeous Persians, but being a cat lover all cats are gorgeous to me. We went out for a pub lunch in nearby Denton, we had a fantastic meal and a fantastic first date, Debbie had never been married but had been in a long term relationship, and here was I married twice and looking for the third, or so it seemed. Debbie was what I would call posh, using strange words like Grarse and glarse, whereas I said Grass and glass. I even tried to hide my rough dialect but she did love it and sometimes had difficulty in understanding some of my phrases. The evening ended well and I drove back to Chesterfield. We arranged to meet again on the Wednesday March the 5th rather a significant date as it was the 19th anniversary of the miners' strike and Grantham was well known as the homing area for the metropolitan police that were policing the picket lines. I went again as planned on the Wednesday and had another wonderful evening, however things moved a little rapidly and I went back again on the Friday and never went back to the flat, I was moving in, I know what you're thinking, this is a recipe for disaster. Well you were wrong, don't ask me what it was but we both knew that we had been waiting for each other all our lives. It seemed too good to be true, but nevertheless we both went into it with our eyes wide open. Debbie showed love and compassion that I had never ever experienced before and for the first time in my life I was relaxed, it was if we had always been together and had just been apart for a while. If you have been fortunate enough to have enjoyed the same then you will know exactly what I mean. Before long I arranged to take her to Bruges on the P&O ferry from Hull we both enjoyed this immensely and got to know each other even better. In knew this was right and so did Debbie and within weeks were arranging to get married. Yes I know I am already married technically, so off to the Solicitors to organise a divorce, and yes I know it would be my second divorce. Such a shame that BOGOF offers were not available then. I was settling in very well but was struggling with the getting up at 4am to drive to Leeds, do a day's work then drive back to Grantham, a 180 mile round trip, and it was a killer. I heard that another ecycle site within the organisation was going to be opened at their Leicester site. I went to see my manager and informed him of my situation and that I wanted a transfer to Leicester. He wasn't happy at this at all, he tried everything to try to dissuade me from leaving and to be honest I didn't really want to, it was purely for logical and economic reasons. Anyhow under sufferance he did arrange for me to go for an interview at the Leicester factory. He still tried putting me off by saying that the manager there was not popular with the workforce and wasn't easy going. That was a red rag to a bull as far as I was concerned. Working with 850 miners where ninety percent of them wanted you dead, tells you that I am not averse to working in difficult conditions.

I went to Leicester for the interview with the factory manager. He was an ex air force officer and had an I'm better than you attitude about him. I was shown round the factory and was introduced to the team who had volunteered to work on my section. I was left to give them a talk and demonstration of what the work was going to be like. The leading hand was telling me how everybody in the factory hated the manager, when I enquired as to why that was he said it was because he had no man management skills, he spoke to people with disrespect and had no understanding of what disabled peoples challenges were.

I went back to the manager's office to finalise the process, he then went into his spiel.

(Manager) "Let me just make one thing clear before you agree to come here, I don't want you or ecycle at my factory".

(Me) "Well, what am I supposed to say to that, at the end of the day the Company has decided to install ecycle here not me, you need someone to manage that who has experience of working on white goods and that is me".

(Manager) "This operation will fail, I will make sure of that!"

(Me) "Well that's not a good basis to start our working relationship, I have no choice but to transfer here simply because of logistics, but I will of course have to speak to the area manager about our conversation, it seems that there will be a problem with that or more like you have a problem with that".

(Manager) "It's nothing to do with the area manager, I am the manager of this site, and I will decide who and what works here, I

have a good working relationship with everybody here and
ecycle coming here will highlight this site to the business,
I don't need that, we are happy with the work we have".

(Me) "Happy! The guys out there hate you and I can tell that
they're scared of you, that's no way to run a factory".

(Manager) "So you're a manager now are you? you say that they hate
me, they can't hate me as you put it, I have never had a
grievance raised against me yet".

(Me) "Well, I want to make this work, but the grievance situation
will change if there are problems".

(Manager) "Well we will see how it goes then, I sense that you could
be trouble, but everyone speaks highly of you so you must
have something, as far as I am concerned this conversation
is off the record".

(Me) "Ok suits me".

I left the site and headed off home, I could sense that this guy was
going to be trouble and would have to be on my guard. I decided to mention
it to the area manager as I had a good working relationship with him.

I and Debbie were engaged to be married very quickly, we planned
the wedding and honeymoon to a T, and everything was based on my
Solicitor's expectation of the divorce coming through. So we planned
everything around that, the marriage was to be on the second of January
2004 followed by the honeymoon to Egypt on the 4th of January. As with
all best laid plans, it didn't quite work out that way. The divorce was not
through by then so we finished up going on honeymoon before we got
married, the wedding was rescheduled for 28th February when we were
assured that everything will be fine by then.

Ken was to be my best man, and against my better judgement Debbie
wanted me to invite my dad. I knew that he would not come, it's been
nearly twenty years since I spoke to him, and I suppose would have been
an ideal way to start to rebuild a relationship but in my heart of hearts
I knew it would not happen. I was in a way glad really because it would
have meant my mother would have to come as well and she was the last
person I wanted there. So the wedding went ahead with nobody from my
side of the family present except close friends, My Boss managed to come

despite recovering after an operation to try and cure his cancer. Steve and his family were there too so I was content. All the other guests were mainly Debbie's friends and mutual friends we had made whilst being together. By now this was obviously my third marriage and there was nobody at any of those except for my dear departed Grandma. This one was different to the others in as much as Debbie was very different from the others, her love was more genuine from the start, and she was constantly telling me she loved me which was new territory for me. What made it special was that I could tell it was genuine.

CHAPTER 20

The twentieth anniversary of the strike

The weekend came and along with it came the local fair, I and Debbie decided to go to the fair which is held in the streets of Grantham. I went on the octopus ride and ended up cracking a rib, this meant that my start at Leicester would be delayed by a couple of weeks.

When I did start back, my new manager was telling me that he wanted 20 machines ready for sale by the weekend. He had promised one of our charity shop customers that amount. I felt that he had done that deliberately thinking that it couldn't be done because the staff were not yet trained, it wasn't a problem as I did that amount at Scottish Power daily. Due to the worn out nature the machines it took me two days, I had the team watching me and I was describing what I was doing to help with training. On the Wednesday I had the team in the training room going over the basic theory when in marches the manager asking to see me outside. I deliberately kept him waiting a few minutes. I went outside.

(Manager) "You don't have time for this, I have arranged another order for twenty machines for another charity shop"

(Me) "well, you see, it's the chicken and egg situation, you cannot have skilled staff without doing the training first, I am not going to put them working until they have a basic understanding of what these machines are and how they work"

(Manager)	"Then you will have to do them"
(Me)	"That would make forty machines in one week, there are seven sites doing ecycle and none of them have ever done forty machines in a week"
(Manager)	"You're such a hot shot engineer, see to it"
(Me)	"I think you made that order deliberately to set me up to fail, there is no way you're going to get another twenty machines in two and a half days"
(Manager)	"I cannot cancel the order, you will have to do them"
(Me)	"Ok I still speak to the area manager, we need to get this sorted"
(Manager)	"Ok He's here next week we will talk to him then"
(Me)	"Well I will talk to him today". With that I returned to the training room to continue the training, the leading hand said that I would have a constant battle with him, I told him that if he wants to fight then I will get him sorted out by his boss.

The following week the area manager came, he took me to one side and told me that my manager had a reputation for being difficult especially to people who he perceived as being a threat. He said that the manager perceived me as a threat and obstructive. I told him that I wasn't a threat but he made it clear he didn't want me or ecycle at his site, which means that my life is going to be difficult, he talks to people like something he had just stepped in, and I am not going to put up with that from him or anyone else. The area manager told me that there were plans to get rid of him and it would take about a year, but to keep that secret. I agreed to try and ignore him and his bullying tactics but I would find it difficult, however I will defend myself and my team. We left it at that and I agreed to call him should anything happen before confronting my manager.

About this time I got a call from a national newspaper on my mobile. The reporter said that he wanted to do an interview with me about the miners' strike as it was now twenty years on. I told him that I wasn't interested. He then told me that they had interviewed my dad and he had said some things that I wouldn't be happy about. With that I agreed to speak to them the transcript from the interview is as follows.

EXCLUSIVE: THE FAMILIES STILL SPLIT BY PIT STRIKE.

I've refused to speak to my son for 20 years. A scab is no son of mine;

IAN Whyles comes up here on most days. The 67-year-old ex-miner borrows his neighbour's collie and trudges up the hill to where the colliery at Whitwell once stood.

Everything's changed now. The Derbyshire pit, which once produced 10,000 tonnes of coal a week, is a muddy wasteland today. The winding gear has gone, the metal gates have been pulled down, the mine shafts plugged with concrete.

But even though the place is virtually unrecognisable, the memories still flood back.

It was here, 20 years ago, that Ian last exchanged words with his son Stephen. He watched in disbelief as his son - then aged 22 - rode through the picket line, escorted by police inside a wire-meshed bus.

"My heart sank," he remembers, looking towards the scrap yard where the gates used to stand. "I couldn't believe my son was on that bus with those other scabs.

"I told him not to do it, to think again, that after all this was over he could still walk down the street with his head held high. But he wouldn't listen. From that day I had nothing to do with him again. A son who's a scab is no son of mine."

For father-of-four Ian, and many other ex-miners in Whitwell, near Worksop, the only thing left from the glory days of coal is bitterness.

Twenty years on, once-close families are still divided and friendships destroyed.

Ian was among 800 miners from Whitwell who went on strike in March 1984 in response to Margaret Thatcher's bid to shut 20 pits around the country.

The year-long strike saw battles between miners and police, pitted miner against miner and plunged thousands of families into poverty.

As the dispute dragged on, many returned to work. At Whitwell half were back by Christmas, and when the strike ended in March 1985, only 74 remained out.

Ian's son Stephen was the 14th miner to return to work. Ever since that day, his wife Muriel and their daughter Rachel, 31, and youngest son

David, 34, have had no contact with him. When their other son, Robert, 44, did speak to Stephen - he was cut off, too.

With a resigned shrug, Stephen - now 41 - says he's given up any hope of making peace. At his home in Grantham, Lincs, he admits: "It still hurts a lot. Before the strike my dad and I were very close. He'd always be there for me. He was a good dad, at least up until the strike.

"He felt ashamed to have a son who was a scab. He kept telling me 'you can't cross a picket line'. "But I was about to get married and had a baby on the way and I'd just agreed a mortgage.

"I was living with my parents at the time. But when I told him I was going to work, he said he wouldn't have a scab living under the same roof.

"So I had to move in with my fiancée's family. My dad stopped talking to my brother Robert when he found we'd started speaking.

"My dad is very much head of the family and now I have no contact with the rest of my family. The last time I saw my mum was years ago in the Co-op. She saw me and just dashed out. It's ridiculous, you can't let things like that destroy your family."

STEPHEN, now manager of an employment firm, says he's offered an olive branch many times - but his dad has always spurned them.

He says: "In 1991 my marriage was on the rocks and I really needed my mum and dad. I sent him a Christmas card, trying to make the first move. But I later heard it went straight on the fire.

"After that I sent him a card explaining why my marriage had broken up. But I didn't get any response."

And last month, he sent Ian an invitation to his wedding - which went in the bin.

Back in Whitwell, Ian says: "It was his third marriage. I hadn't gone to any of the others, so why should I go to this one? If he didn't want his dad to disown him, he should have thought twice before going back to work."

For Ian Whyles, The passing years will not change his mind.

He admits: "Yes, I'm bitter. My wife's bitter. But I've no regrets. It could have been different, but only if my son hadn't gone back to work.

"Maybe on my deathbed I'll speak to him again. I'll call him a bloody scab and then I'll die."

That piece was in the paper across the centre pages. That morning when I walked into the factory, there were lots of the workers looking at the paper, there were nudges and head nodding as I walked into the canteen to get a cup of tea.

I noticed that they had got a copy of the paper, there was the article with the picture of me and my dad stuck on the canteen wall.

No sooner had I arrived in the canteen the manager came in and got himself a cup of tea then asked me to follow him into his office.

After we got to his office, he asked me about the article, I told him about going back to work. He asked me how I felt about the article. I told him that I wasn't happy and that there were a few misquotes although nothing major. He told me that he held me in a different light, he told me that he had got me wrong to a degree and admired what I did during the strike. He told me he had submitted the article to HR to see what they thought of it. I told him that at the end of the day it was twenty years ago and not really anybody else's business.

He was worried about the union's reaction, I told him I had a good relationship with the union steward on site but I would speak to him. He told me the sooner I did that the better and that he knew I would be trouble but was laughing. He offered his hand and asked if we could start again. I told him I was happy to do that, but did remind him that I was not the problem.

I left and went to the union shop steward's office, lo and behold he was reading the article, he told me to sit down and close the door, which I did.

(Union) "I see you have quite a history by the looks of this article"

(Me) "yes, and I know you used to work at the pit too"

(Union) "yes I left long before the strike, I think you did what you had to do back then, I might not agree with what you did but I admire the balls you had to do it"

(Me) "Well it was a difficult time for me then but I don't regret it one bit"

(Union) "If my dad had said that about me I would want to kill him, he should be ashamed of himself saying that in a national newspaper"

(Me) "Yes it is unfortunate, but I am proud I haven't once slagged him off once in twenty years and he has resorted to that, still I'm hardened to it now"

(Union) "Don't worry about troops, they won't fully understand what it means but I will help where I can if anyone starts tittle tattling".

(Me) "Cheers, that means a lot"

I went back to my section and again my team were reading the article, there were lots of questions and I answered them as honestly as I could.

Later that day things were very near normal, I received numerous calls from radio stations and newspapers asking for a reaction to the article, I declined all of them. When I got home I was having my tea when the phone rang again, it was Brian Milligan from BBC Breakfast, and he asked me if I would be willing to do a piece for BBC Breakfast. I told him that I didn't want to comment about what my dad had said, he acknowledged the article but said the piece was planned before that. I agreed to talk to him about what he wanted and arranged for him to visit me at home. He arrived a day or two later and explained that it would be an authored piece which meant I would talk over the film. this was to take place at the old pit site and on colliery row where I grew up, I realised that this could serve as a life memento and I would also be able to tell why I went back to work, every newspaper and radio and TV before were not interested in the political reasons just the human effect side of it, that is with the exception of the BBC, they had never tried to make a drama out of it, they were just interested in facts. With that I decided to trust Brian and go ahead with the piece.

We arranged to meet at the old pit site in Whitwell.

We started the filming and I was quite shocked how reliving it was quite hairy, standing on that pit bridge again and recalling my thoughts and emotions was quite evocative. It literally transported me back in time. To think that something that happened twenty years ago could still be as evocative and fresh in one's memory shows just how harrowing the experience was. I am not one for over emphasising something at all, I was just more aware of the impact on my life the strike actually had and is still having today to some degree.

I watched the interview when it aired the following morning, it was edited very well I thought, Brian had portrayed it exactly as it was done.

Back at work most of the staff saw the interview including my manager, the response was surprising in as much everyone was in support, which was a relief.

I have since done interviews for BBC radio 2, radio 4 and BBC radio 5live. The radio 2 interview was a live one that was nerve racking to say the least.

Later that week I was contacted by a Worksop local newspaper, they said that my dad had been in touch with them wanting to retract the statements he made about me in the national newspaper. I told him that I had nothing to say to them except that if my dad wanted to retract his remarks he can do so in the national newspaper where he made them not a local one. They were desperate to persuade me but I declined.

What I didn't know at the time was that my dad had received a bit of stick about the remarks in the village because there were miners living in the village that went back to work and my dad talks to them as if nothing had happened. So now the jigsaw fitted together, he obviously wanted to retract the comments to the local paper so that only the locals would see it. He being a councillor made his position a little sticky. No retraction was made in the national newspaper, he obviously meant his remarks but didn't count on the adverse reaction from his peers. My dignity has remained intact throughout, I would never ever make hurtful and disrespectful remarks about my dad to the press or media even if I had any remarks of that kind to make. I was hurt about the remarks and still am today, I am ashamed of him as a father but he is entitled to his opinions and I respect that, but nothing else, he is no better than my so called mother now.

THE DAILY MIRROR CENTRE PAGE HEADLINE

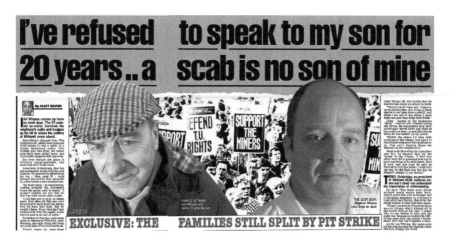

I've refused 20 years.. a to speak to my son for scab is no son of mine

EXCLUSIVE: THE FAMILIES STILL SPLIT BY PIT STRIKE

COURTESY OF THE DAILY MIRROR

CHAPTER 21

The aftermath

The ecycle business was doing reasonably well, we were well into doing refrigeration by this time I had managed to get Ken a job, my good friend from Scottish Power, and he had been working at the Leeds site in and off. I wanted to secure him a position at Leicester because I needed a good experienced engineer as I couldn't be there all the time. Ken was the one guy I could depend on and I sold that well to the area manager much to the annoyance of the factory manager, which was another good reason to have Ken on board. My manager was upset that I had approached the area manager directly rather than going through him. The truth is I couldn't trust him to sell it to him, he wouldn't want what he perceived to be an ally of mine at the site. What he didn't know then however is that Ken is not confrontational by nature, but if he lost it the best option was to get out of his way. I was always secretly hoping that the manager would rub ken up the wrong way, it came close a few times but Ken was happy for me to battle with the manager.

Battle is the right word, one particular day we had a load of fridge freezers that had been repaired but were awaiting cleaning, cleaning was always the bottleneck in the process. We had urgent orders for refrigeration. I was off site for a couple of days doing an internal course, when I came back I noticed the refrigeration waiting for cleaning had gone. The manager had arranged for the charity shop that they were sold to, to pick them up whilst

I wasn't there. When the products arrived at the shop the manager of the charity shop quite rightly complained at the dirty and smelly condition these appliances were in. My manager called me into the office saying that I had sent these out to the shop, I was in charge of the section so therefore I was responsible. I put it to him that he had arranged this and in my view deliberately to stitch me up. He had a snide grin on his face just like a cheeky kid that had just watched a prank come off. We had very strong words, one of his famous quotes was always "off the record I want to say this". At one of his off the record moments I told him that on or off the record if he tried stitching me up again He would be shoving his lunch up his arse to eat it because thats how far down I would knock his shiny white teeth. Obviously he reported me to the area manager and HR, As a result I raised a formal counter grievance against him for extreme provocation. I admitted I may have sounded threatening but never admitted the exact phrase. Ironically though he was the one in hot water because when I was asked to prove the provocation the area manager jumped in chapter and verse with all the reports I had made to him. My disciplinary was dropped but his hasty departure would be ever quicker now.

In public such as area meetings with ecycle he was always singing my praises. But in private he was always trying to get one over on me.

I approached him one day with an idea that I had, I told him that I had contacts within a major white goods manufacturer and could secure us a good deal to buy all their returns at cost price and less in some cases, I knew this because I had been in talks. Prior to this to see if it was feasible. My manager agreed that working with clapped out ten year old machines was not the way to earn money. I approached our area manager with the idea and it excited him, He asked me to set up a meeting with the manufacturer. I set the meeting up and arranged for myself and the Company buyer to go to the meeting. At that meeting it was made clear that it was only because of my relationship with their reps that I had that got us in there. The meeting went well and the buyer made all the right noises with all sorts of promises, they even offered to sell the spare parts to us at 40% of cost. I left the two sides to do all the behind the scenes stuff, but for weeks the manufacturer was ringing me and sending me emails asking what the hell was going on, they had no contact from senior management since the initial introduction. They had two articulated Lorries at Southampton docks waiting for the word to deliver them. The management totally disrespected the manufacturer by not even returning emails, all I could get out of them was that they couldn't get authorisation to purchase them, so why didn't they communicate that? Truth is, the Company only played at business and were never any good at securing decent contracts, this one frightened them because of the numbers. However my contact at the manufacturer told me in no uncertain terms that I had wasted his time and made him look a fool with his bosses and that he wanted nothing more to do with me. So Thanks, I have now lost a good friend and contact because of your ineptness. This deal would have been very profitable for us and moreover would have supplied our customers with quality appliances, and less callouts to repairs than at present. All it took was a phone call to say it was a no go, but the way of this outfit was to just ignore them and hope that they would get fed up. This was an expensive lesson learned for me in terms of friendships and good contacts.

One particular day, I was in charge of the factory when I was called into reception by one of the shop floor staff that was standing in for the receptionist. I went there I was told that I had some visitors in the waiting area, I opened the door and found a camera crew and reporter there from a local TV network wanting me to comment on the twentieth anniversary of the miners' strike. Politely but firmly showed them out of the door, not least for the fact that the Company did not allow TV crews or reporters onto the premises. I was amazed. They didn't want my view twenty years on they just wanted my reaction to the newspaper article. When I got home that night I was met with a TV camera crew from the same network on my drive waiting and with a small crowd of onlookers. The neighbours must have wondered what the hell they wanted with me. Sent them packing again but had to physically remove a tripod from my driveway. I was in the kitchen later making a cup of tea with the TV on in the background when I heard my dad's name mentioned on the local news. He had given them an interview but said very little that made any sense other than how marvellous the soup kitchen women were during the strike. That in my mind was a public relations exercise to try and improve his image after the newspaper debacle.

I was looking on the internet and researching my name as one does and was astonished to find that I had done interviews in Australia, Canada and

America. Obviously they had either bought or copied the interview I had done locally. Below is a transcript from the Australian version.

REPORTER: Twenty-five years ago this week a miners' strike began in the UK. It became one of the political events which defined the prime ministership of Margaret Thatcher.

It divided the country and led to the downfall of one of the country's biggest trade unions. The yearlong strike pitted the police against the miners and it also split families and mates; a quarter of a century on and that bitterness still runs deep.

REPORTER: The dispute started with the walkout of a Yorkshire mining pit on the 5th of March 1984. The strike was led by the mining union boss Arthur Scargill and it quickly spread throughout the mining industry.

REPORTER: The strike also caused divisions among miners themselves. Some were unhappy that Arthur Scargill had not called a ballot.

Steve Whyles was in the midst of the strike for six months, but eventually when no national ballot was called he went back to work and crossed the picket line.

STEVE WHYLES: Well that's a decision that will stay with me for the rest of my life; it's not the easiest of things to do. I can remember when the bus first pulled up outside my girlfriend's house, and I saw the weld mesh all the way round it, and the driver and his mate had got crash helmets on; that was very intimidating.

And then getting on the bus you felt your palpitations thumping, and then as you began to settle down you approached the pit, and then when the bus got to the brow of the bridge and I saw hundreds upon hundreds of pickets, bloody angry ones at that sheez that was horrendous.

People were shouting and yelling 'scab', 'Judas'. There were about five deep on either side of the road all the way down to the pit yard, it was the scariest experience I have ever had before or since.

REPORTER:	Was your Father on the picket?
STEVE WHYLES:	Yes, my dad, was on the picket line and a lot friends too. That's the derision it caused. You either went with the mob rule or you stuck firm to what you believed in and voted with your feet. There was no halfway, it was one or the other. You know if you've got principles and you firmly believe in them, then you have to stick by them, whether the main consensus thinks it's right or wrong.
REPORTER:	And he never quite reconciled with his father.
STEVE WHYLES:	True, we haven't hardly spoken at all since then.
REPORTER:	Your dad has said that a son who is a scab is no son of his, how does that make you feel?
STEPHEN WHYLES:	I believe he said that yes, he has since tried to retract that comment and others. There has to be a cost, I suppose, and the cost to me was the family split, which by and large is still prevalent today. It is the only regret I have.

I was hoping that this would be it, I could have easily have had a go at my dad through the media, but that wouldn't have served any purpose whatsoever.

Some Months went by when it was announced at work that the Manager would be leaving, it cost the Company Â£20,000 to get rid of him but in my view it was money well spent.

The next manager was a young man and an Australian, he was a university graduate and it was soon clear that he had a good sound business sense, although his ideas were logical and made good business sense, the figures were really unachievable for a number of reasons. He lasted about a year before the next manager was to come in, lo and behold it was to be my old manager from Leeds, talk about irony. He seemed a good manager to have on the surface but never came across as being interested. The good thing about that was I was left to run my section my way within reason and was given a purchase card with its own budget. He relied heavily on me to run the section and did have some useful input. He was always critical of the area manager and thought that all he did was drive around the country doing nothing. Despite his resentment of me leaving Leeds we did seem to get on very well, or for now at least.

My marriage to Debbie was going very well. She was comfortable with the media attention around the miners' strike and was very supportive. I know deep down she would rather my life was not played out on TV and in the press.

She had a close relationship with her Mother and Sister's, one of her sisters had MS. And a cruel form it was too, she was fully dependant on carers as she was unable to walk. This was the first time I had come across this type of illness and couldn't help thinking that no matter how bad a blow you might think life has served you, it could be a hell of a lot worse. Debbie was totally dedicated to making her sisters life a little bit more bearable, and although useless as far as helping practically was concerned I was happy to be around her. She was coping with this dreadful disease very well and was able to have some semblance of a normal life as far as independent living was concerned. I found myself thinking that of all the low life's, murderers, rapists, paedophile's in this world why is it that only decent people seem to get horrific diseases? Life is just not fair. If any of you have anyone in your life who is suffering or you are suffering yourself, you won't need me to tell you how hard it is.

In 2008 the Company announced its modernisation programme after the government announced it was going to eventually withdraw financial support or at least at the same level's. The organisation had over 80 factories up and down the country at the time and the government funding amounted to about 1 million pounds per factory per year. The Company is the only company that I have come across that budgets to make a loss, the budget was to ONLY lose Â£14,000 per disabled person per year, staggering really, this is tax payer's money they are messing with.

As a result of the modernisation programme over 20 factories were closed and the ones surviving had to produce business plans to show how they intended to increase income. My manager did do this but it was based on false promises and stretching of achievable workloads from our contracts. But it got past the board, no surprise there.

CHAPTER 22

Is the Strike Dead?

So the Company is asking for voluntary redundancies, they were particularly wanting Staff to apply, as I was staff then I will apply for a quote to see what my package will be.

I requested the package and learned that it would be a year's salary plus Â£5000, that was a cracking deal, I applied for a few jobs and was lucky enough to get an interview for a company in Grantham. I then read the procedure for applying for redundancy. The procedure was to notify your manager and if he was happy and had no business reason for denying it then you would be submitted. I took my application through to my Manager and he told me that he would consider it a personal insult for me to apply and would decline the application saying I was key staff. That was utter rubbish it was just him being bloody minded, however I am stuffed. I withdrew my application for the post in Grantham and had to stay put. This was strange as since ecycle finished I was merely wandering round the site without a proper job. The safety officer come Team leader applied for Voluntary redundancy and was accepted, so is not the safety officer role key to any business. In our next staff meeting the manager informed me that I was to be the new safety officer, I asked about the team leader role and he said it would have to be advertised internally. Great my role in ecycle was a team leading role so I would apply for that.

The interviews came along and a guy from Coventry factory applied as well as me so there was just the two of us. As my previous role was a team leading role, and as I was out of a job so to speak and as I was already in situ I considered myself in good stead. My manager was to conduct the interviews along with a guy from HR. To my horror he chose the guy from Coventry. Now I got the picture, he was going to be vindictive and my union rep had already informed me that he resented me from leaving him at Leeds.

When the new guy came to the site I welcomed him as was only right and proper, after all it wasn't his fault the manager was a vindictive arsehole. As it turned out I got on with him extremely well, he was a good down to earth guy, the guys on the shop floor were very angry and upset that I hadn't got the job and did make the new guy's life a little difficult.

I at least new where I stood with the manager although he didn't have the balls to tell me to my face that he held some resentment towards me. Ironically when I started at Leeds I saved this guy his job after the union official raised a grievance against him about something he said in an meeting, The union guy had told me that he had researched the salary for the role we were doing and it should have been Â£2000 more than we were on, He put this to the manager and the manager said that he would like to give us Â£2000 extra per year but there were procedures to follow and it cannot be done just like that. The union guy said in his grievance that he had promised to give us the extra Â£2000. I backed him up because I knew full well that he didn't say that. It was made clear to me during the investigation that my manager could end up losing his position for making promises that he was not authorised to make. I told the investigator the truth and it saved him his job, I could have lied and got rid of him and got Â£2000 extra per year for my trouble. I am happy that I didn't forgo my morals for the sake of a few quid, but I would like to think that I would have remembered something like that if the situation was reversed. My relationship with him was going downhill. The higher up he got the further distanced he became from the people that put him there. Sure I am angry and disappointed but at least I knew where I stood with him. The only positive thing about him really was that he did show empathy with the disabled employees, but so he should as he is disabled himself.

The Manager was now moving on as he was successful in applying for the area Manager role, the role that had previously been made redundant. I told him that he could now drive round the country doing nothing, he thought that was funny going by the embarrassed laugh he gave. So we are to get yet another new Manager at Leicester. The next Manager was a guy from Stoke-On-Trent, he seemed a nice guy very down to earth and seemed sincere, I told him on his walk site visit that Managers at this site only last a few months and not to take his coat off, he laughed saying that he was only expecting six months anyway.

When he was at the site full time I got on very well with him, he wasn't a strong man and didn't know how to handle confrontation.

One of our major contract customers had lost faith in the new team leader, they thought he was incompetent and they told our Manager that they didn't want him anywhere near their work. This posed a problem for the manager as he couldn't have a team leader that couldn't get involved with a contract that was ninety percent of our work. He decided to take him off the shop floor and have him as his aide, and I would have to stand in as Team leader, I told him in no uncertain terms that I was not going to do that. He pointed out that I was already doing most of his work such as personal development plans for the employees and that I always took control in the absence of the manager or team leader. That may well be the case but I wasn't going to do something that the previous manager and now area manger deemed me unsuitable for. Good old dependable Steve he will take the reins, well er No! This was a problem for the area manager to solve and he was to pay a visit to the site to try and sort it out.

So the area manager came to the site and it was arranged for the Manager of the Company we had the contract with to be in the meeting, the meeting got underway and before long I was summoned into the meeting room. the manager told me that the customer wanted to deal with either me or the leading hand, and refused to allow the team leader anywhere near their product. The area manager asked me to accompany him outside, making the excuse that I could go to the smoke shed for a cigarette. Once there he said,

"I thought you had ambitions of management and managing your own site"?

(Me)   "I have, very much so"
(Manager) "Then this is your opportunity to shine and show the
            Company what you are capable of, I know what this is

about, you are sore at not getting the team leader job in the first place".

(Me) "Damn right it is, whilst ever you are area manager I will never get on, that much is clear, you employed this guy when it was not logical to do so, but you did it purely to keep me back, that's my opinion and I won't alter from that".

(Manager) "He was employed because his previous manager would have been very happy to get rid of him because he wasn't popular there either".

(Me) "So you employed him knowing full well that he might not be suitable just as a favour to another manager, I challenge you to give an instance when I have shown to be incompetent in my role? Yet you employed him over me when it was neither logical nor logistical to do so".

(Manager) "I think that your readiness to be confrontational without seeing the bigger picture is one of your main sticking points, you are excellent with the teams, they all like you that much is very clear, to me you are better suited in your current role and then maybe next time you would be in better stead for a managerial role".

(Me) "I think you have just justified my being confrontational as you put it, I only lock horns with people when I see blatant wrong doings especially when it involves management, not because I like to go head long into battle with management, but because if management don't do what's in the best interest if the site and its people, then I will object, that's always been my way, I'm no extremist on a crusade, I just do and act on what I think is right, and apart from all that I regarded us as friends, especially since that incident in Leeds with the union, I saved your neck then, not because I wanted to court favour but because it was the right thing to do, I could have lied with the other two and be two thousand pounds a year better off and with you off the scene, but I didn't much to the annoyance of the union".

(Manager) "thats my point, this attitude of yours is against the best interest of the site and its people, you cannot hold grudges and grievances over what's gone before, you have to move

	on, it's immature, so how about it? Take over the role along with your current role, it will show the board that you ate management material".
(Me)	"You just don't get it do you? What is he going to do then if we are not swapping roles, er umm let me guess, he's going to carry on being the mangers deputy and being in prime position when the manager's role comes up again, further more I haven't heard any offers of remuneration for doing it".
(Manager)	"You are already above the remuneration for the team leader role so it's impossible to pay you anymore"
(Me)	"Well that just sums it up, you want me to do my role and the team leader's role without any consideration or acknowledgement, my answer still remains, see ya"

With that I went back inside leaving him there. That takes the biscuit for me, I don't honestly think I was unreasonable, I have revisited the episode many times and have come to the same conclusion. This guy had a very short memory yet thought me unreasonable for not going along with his plans just to make life easier for him.

I can however see how immature it looks from the management point of view, but I have morals and a strong belief in doing what I consider to be right, I can't help that, it's the way I am. As the miners' strike has taught me, if I went with what other people wanted me to do and disregard procedures, law and fundamentals, then perhaps my life would have been easier but it certainly wouldn't let me rest easy in my bed. If I don't stick to my principles now then the last twenty odd years of the miners' strike and the split from my family as such would have counted for nothing. The one thing I learned from my experience with my Mother at an early age was that I would have to defend myself and stand up for myself, its maybe because of that experience that I am the way I am, she is certainly responsible for my being against wrong doing and the bullying of people less able to defend themselves.

The factory mulled on slowly and I ended up doing most of the team leader role by default, I couldn't bring myself to tell the workers that it wasn't my job when they came to me with an issue they had, because I knew full well they would just walk away and suffer in silence rather than take it to the team leader.

Soon the manager was to leave and we would be getting yet another manager, this time a guy from Oldham, he was ok to a point until one day a few months into his role at Leicester he called me into his office and the following ensued.

(Manager) "Steve, it hasn't escaped my notice that you are ambitious and keen to get into management, I know from experience the best way into management in this company is through project management, I am going away on holiday for ten days and I want to give you a project, if successful it will show the board what you can do".

(Me) "Is there an echo in here? I seemed to have heard this speech before, it will just end up with management pissing up my back again".

(Manager) "That's my point, this will show what you can do with some responsibility and a chance to save the Company a lot of money"

(Me) "Well let's hear it, no harm in that I suppose".

(Manager) "We are spending about £30,000 per year on outsourcing engineering, our customer as you know requires us to mill our own stainless steel plates, it is expensive, while I am away I want you to source a milling machine for us capable of cutting stainless steel and bring it in under £25,000. The Company will support purchases of equipment if the money can be recovered in 12 months".

(Me) "yes, I see the logic, but that's not gonna be easy".

(Manager) "I'm not saying it will be easy but nothing is in management, if you pull this off you will have something concrete to put to management the next time you put yourself forward, do you see where I'm coming from"?

(Me) "Yes, of course I do"

(Manager) "Then you'll do it"?

(Me) "Well I will give it a go, sure".

(Manager) "one other thing, keep it to yourself until you are successful, if the team leader and leading hand get wind of what we are up to they could tip off the engineer".

(Me) "Ok"

(Manager) "I will visit the Company where you source the mill from when I return and pay him, this will be entirely on your back, it will let you experience stress in management, and no, I'm not pissing up your back as you put it, I want to see what you can do, so I can help you progress in the Company".

(Me) "That will never happen while we have the current area manager, he has a resentment of me".

(Manager) "I can deal with him, I know I have people in higher places than him, and even he can't fail to notice a good result".

(Me) "Ok, let's do it"

(Manager) "You can start when you like, just keep on top of the health and safety stuff etc., don't let it take over from your current role".

(Me) "Ok"

To cut a very long story short, I sourced a milling machine with a special drill bit attachment for cutting the stainless steel plates and would do so in batches of ten at a time, the supplier purchased the drill bits in our behalf, he arranged for a programmer to program the mill, a training session to train our internal engineer and delivery and installation. All for a mere £9,000. I told him my budget was £10,000.

When the manager returned off his holiday I told him that I had not only succeeded in my quest but had excelled it for a lot less than half of the budget, all it needed now was for him to visit the supplier and see the deal for himself and arrange for payment. He made excuse after excuse, asking me to rearrange the appointment, time and time again. The supplier eventually told me that I had cost time and money in preparing the machine and never had any intentions of purchasing the machine at all, he didn't believe my explanation at all. I remonstrated with my manger over it as I was very angry, not so much that I had been made to look an idiot but that I had wasted a good guy's time and resources albeit in good faith, and now my reputation in the community was worthless, the supplier was a very big business in the Leicester area. It turned out that my manager was not interested because he was told he was moving on to manage another site nearer to his home.

CHAPTER 23

The end of an Era

So I was left with egg on my face again. This is becoming like ground hog day, another manager out and another one in. The next manager was a woman, makes a change after all the men have made a pig's ear of it so far so why not a woman. The new manager visited the site and she was from the Liverpool area, she seemed quite bubbly and friendly and very much down to earth, she had worked her way up from the shop floor so that was different.

Initially she would stay in a local hotel rather than travel each day, this in itself was different, all previous managers that came from a fair distance away tended to travel to and from the factory in work time which meant that they were only on site for around 5 hours each day at best.

It soon became clear that Suzanne the new Manager was a hands on manager that too was new, she would readily get her hands dirty, so at last a manager that led by example now that is novel, what's more because she came up from the shop floor she had a good understanding of the challenges the disabled workforce faced.

One of her first decisions was to take the management team out of their offices and put us in a communal office, this didn't go down well with any of us, least of all me. Still, she went ahead with it anyway and before long IT were on site rerouting all the comms and computers. So very soon we were settled in our new place, before too long I began to see the advantages not least the communication between the management team was a lot better, relationships between us improved also. The only downside was the receptionist, she was in there too. She was one to watch she was a known stirrer, a typical tittle tattler and she soon planted herself as the factory spy, and informing the manager on silly things, for instance one day one of the team was playing games on the pc, she promptly went into the hallway between the communal office and the manager's office and. Said "I don't know how you get away with it" in such a higher toned voice that the manager wouldn't be able to miss the comment, but when she was constantly looking at hotels and holiday resorts then obviously that was different. Very soon we the management team soon learned to use this to our advantage, we often dropped red herrings in conversation which always got to Suzanne faster than the speed of light.

I had a particularly good relationship with Suzanne, she was always true to her word and respected my opinion, she was always quick to commend me on the health and safety performance and she would always listen to advice. her only downside was that she couldn't see the receptionist for what she was, she was always saying she didn't like kiss asses but the receptionist was the biggest kiss ass on site, and the biggest critic of Suzanne, well after the team leader that is, he and Suzanne were constantly battling and always in public, quite entertaining really. For once we had a manger that was extremely aware of her surroundings and more to the point one that didn't see me as a threat. She knew of the difficulties I had had with some of the previous managers and understood too seemingly. Her sexuality was always in question with us and we would often have debates on this, the overall consensus was that she was a lesbian although we never had cast iron proof and to be honest it didn't really matter whether she was or not, she was a decent manager and that was what really mattered. We would rather have a lesbian than an arsehole and we have had plenty of those.

This particular time was difficult as the government had announced that The Company would have funding removed and would have to be self-sustaining in the next eighteen months or so. That was a joke the vast majority of the Company factories other than automotive didn't stand a chance in hell of being self-sustaining, the history of the funding was that the government gave the Company £25,000 per disabled capita per year.

The most we had ever earned was around £1700 in a week, mostly however we barely did that amount per month. In reality it was worse than that. You don't have to be Einstein to work that out. The Company had 45 factories now after approximately 28 factories were closed in 2008, so if we halved that loss figure to get an average for the Company that would mean that the Company as a whole was losing far too much money per week. On the flip side of that was how much it would cost the tax payer in benefits to over 3000 disabled people. I suspect that it would be a better option to keep the factories open if not least for moral reasons as in real terms it would cost the tax payer less, and the disabled people would at least be contributing and have a feeling of belonging. In most cases the Company was the only life they knew and to pull that away would have a devastating effect I suspect.

True to the Company's fashion, our manager would soon be on her way off to another site, it would be better to install a conveyor belt in the manager's office rather than office furniture. This time I was going to apply, the team leader at the site also was going to apply but at this moment we were the only two and it looked like a two horse race. The only stumbling block was the area manger whom I had a difficult relationship with was to be conducting the interviews. I was nonetheless going to give it a go though. I submitted my application and began work on how I would make the factory more self-sustainable, I did have some ideas but whether they would have been enough let alone successful was anybody's guess. The team leader was doing the same, I felt we had an equal chance. The interviews were arranged and we attended we learned then that there was a third contender, a woman from Coventry factory, I knew her she was my oppo as it were in Coventry, she had a management career before The Company so we were now fearing that we would lose out, the area manager was a bit of Lech in my opinion and she was someone who would be a welcome sight if I can put it that way.

The interviews were arranged to take place at Pontefract factory, which made perfect sense, 90 miles from Leicester, a master stroke when there is the head office only 4 miles from the Leicester factory.

I know it wouldn't have been right to hold them in the Leicester factory, but 90 miles away, what's that all about? It makes good sense to hold the interviews away from the factory in question especially with two of the candidates working there, but 90 miles away when the head office was only 4 miles from the Leicester factory, I would be passing six factories on the way.

The interview day arrived and I did a reasonably good interview or at least I thought I did. The team leader also thought he did quite well, we had no way of knowing how the Coventry candidate did. I remember telling the team leader that it is rare to promote from within the site due to familiarity with the workforce. However it's done now, it's just a matter of waiting.

A week or so later the area manager came on site along with his boss, they asked to see the team leader and later in the day the Coventry candidate appeared on site too. They both went in to what to all intents and purposes was a second interview although they later denied that's what it was. I was not called either for a discussion or to be told I was out of the running. Strange, am I still in with a shot or not?

Speculation was rife within the factory as one would expect, the guys on the shop floor were routing for me which was warming.

The following weekend I was at home when I received a call from the team leader, he said that one of his pals from Coventry had overheard a phone call with Jo the Coventry candidate where it was obvious she had been given the job. I rang the area manager and asked him outright, he denied it, saying that no decision had been made as yet. I suspected he was being his usual deceitful self and telling lies because his lips were moving.

Back at the factory another week passed by when the area manager came to the site, he came to me outside in the smoking area and said that I was unsuccessful, I gave him some verbal's and remonstrated at the way it had been handled. I immediately composed one of my infamous emails and sent it off to HR at the head office stating that I wished to raise an official grievance against the area manager. I also phoned Jo and congratulated her, I told her about the grievance and wanted her to know it was not about her, she went on to deny the alleged phone call but gave very accurate details as to what was supposedly said so I got my confirmation from that, they were all lying through their teeth, ok, it's understandable for Jo she was in an impossible position really.

A representative from HR came to the site and held a meeting with me to start the grievance process off. I notified my union rep who was based at Leeds and the ball was rolling. To cut a long laborious process short my grievance was upheld and I was asked what Would put things right for me, I felt the Manager should have been disciplined, HR said that both managers had been told in no uncertain terms that the process was unfair and that they had appeared to be vindictive even if not deliberate, I told HR that the damage was already done, restarting the process now would serve no one and wouldn't result in a fair process. I told them that I wanted a one to one meeting with the area manager, an off the record meeting where I could give him hell verbally and demand the truth. To my surprise they agreed, I said that manager would not agree, but they said he had no choice.

In the meantime whilst awaiting the manager to contact me for the meeting the new Manager came to the site, she was to be mentored by the existing Manager as part of the handover process. She as expected came over keen and with a plethora of new ideas some good, some not so good. I expected that things could be a little awkward what with me and the team leader applying for the job, I was expecting things to be difficult for me as the new manager was after all an ex safety officer, she to her credit was quick to tell me that she would rely on me heavily in the safety and quality department and would not interfere so long as I did the job satisfactory. As time went on she was always telling me that I was doing a good job but I was always suspicious of her, mainly because of her closeness to the senior managers that I had raised a grievance with. I did not trust them and with obvious good reason.

Meanwhile finally the area manager was back on site again and this time he asked me if I wanted to have the meeting I had requested, I agreed so we went into the conference room where we discussed the fiasco of the selection process. He conceded that it wasn't the best selection process in the world and he acknowledged how it must have looked from my point of view, he also admitted that the telephone call between him and the successful candidate did take place and that she couldn't keep her mouth shut. So in a nutshell he tried to deny my allegations of vindictiveness and that I had been deliberately deselected for the second stage but we both knew that was not the case. It was apparent to me that he had been instructed to pacify me because he was on edge for most of the meeting and was not comfortable in that situation. So it ended with nothing really being solved and in hindsight I should have demanded more at the grievance hearing, both senior managers should have been disciplined in my view but knowing the Company management as I do it was never going to happen.

Very soon the announcement came that all the factories would close and within 12 months. Our factory would be the first to go, the government had withdrawn all funding and The Company would have to be self-sustaining or close. Both senior managers came to the site and the new manager made the announcement to us all and immediately burst into tears leaving one of the senior managers to finish giving the brief. There was to be support provided by means of councillors and the job centre people would visit the site to advice on benefits available and help with CV's etc.

I was not worried personally, I felt that I would soon get another job, I did however need to get my health and safety qualification (NEBOSH NGC) if I was to have a hope of getting another job in health and safety. The manager said she would get me the funding to take the course externally but it wasn't required, The Company were going to run a course internally and the manager got me a place on that. NEBOSH NGC is a notoriously tough exam but I had to pass it or risk having to pay for it myself after I finished at The Company.

The advisors came from the job-centre plus to give us all individual advice, my turn soon cane around where I was told that I would receive £71 per week for six months then absolutely nothing after that because Debbie my wife was working. I remonstrated with the advisors stating that I have worked over 30 years without sponging anything from the state as had Debbie, we were independent people as far as tax and national insurance was concerned yet she was expected to support me financially after the six months, I told the advisor that they could shove it. I found it absolutely disgraceful that a man and his wife who have worked all their life doing the right thing and working and paying their way in society would get no support in their hour of need, yet if you claim benefits all your life you will get your mortgage or rent paid and other needs provided for, I was told that as I wouldn't get any help with my mortgage I would need to contact my mortgage provider, as if You inform them early rather than when you cannot pay your mortgage they will help you. Ok that gives a little comfort, So Debbie phoned Santander who we had our mortgage with only to be told that they cannot help and if the mortgage fell into arrears then we risked having our home repossessed. So it was abundantly clear that there is no such thing as help for the working men and women of this country when they fall on hard times but if you are work shy seemingly you will be looked after. This country is running arse over tit, it's time to pay a visit to my local MP and give him some serious grief.

CHAPTER 24

The final Months

So the appointment is made I was now to see my MP on Saturday morning at 10 o'clock. Not really sure that it will do any good but I want to have my say anyway.

The day of the meeting had arrived I went to the council offices in central Grantham and was waiting there at 10 minutes to ten for the appointment to start at 10 o'clock. I sat there in the waiting room until 10:15 when he finally turned up saying "are you early or am I late"? I said "you are late, I was on time". We started the meeting by telling me that he had read my letter and he understood where I was coming from. He said he appreciated me taking the time to contact him and would help if he could. I told him about the government decision to close The Company and that my salary had been frozen for the past three years because I was earning over £21000, per year. Now I was thrown onto the scrap heap with limited income support for a maximum of six Months. Furthermore if I had debts over £15000 the government would be able to help me or at least an external agency would. I asked him why it was that a person born and bred in this country and had worked all his life and contributed to the country by paying his way for over thirty years would be treated with contempt, and why is it that because I have not recklessly amassed debts that I was never realistically going to pay, I cannot get help. Yet if I had done the opposite, everyone would bend over backwards to help, arse over tit indeed. He replied by saying that the country was on its knees thanks to the Labour government previously, there was no money for basic needs hence the cost cutting methods utilised by the present government, I told him that in my view it was not all down to the labour party, sure, they didn't help matters especially when they bailed out Northern Rock but the real problem is immigration we are taking thousands of immigrants into this country giving them benefits, council houses etc. yet the working people of this country that have done all the contributing can't get a brass farthing.

The meeting was never going to give me any answers, he was full of shit like most politicians they take the most out of the people they regard less. The working men and women of this country are just cash cows to the government whether Tory or Labour.

He ended by asking me to make another appointment to see him in six Months' time, I somehow think I won't bother but It's the last time I vote for any of the main parties in future maybe I will try UKIP they sound appealing. Don't get me wrong, I am not racist, in fact I have many friends from all over the world Asians, Africans, Americans Australians you name it, but when every second person you pass speaks eastern European like they do in my home town, then its time something was done, and I know I'm only saying what most people are thinking. My last political spout here is that my view is that immigrants are mostly responsible for the demise of our benefits system, housing crisis and the NHS. I know that view is not publicly accepted but it is my view, if you come here and can pay your way then you are welcome, if not, then bugger off back from whence you came. If I was to jump on a plane and get off in a European country then tell immigration that I was here to claim off their state, I would be on the next plane back.

Back at the factory our Manager was telling us all that it was business as usual and that nothing had changed, and that as part of the management team it was our job to portray that message to the workers. Good business sentiment but hardly realistic or compassionate to the disabled workforce, some of whom had been in The Company in excess of thirty years. The most pressing need was to help them and try to make them less worried about the future. Like the politicians though I don't have any answers for them, I cannot tell them that everything will be ok, I had one of the guys ask me that when he gets his money and the factory closes, how long will it be before he can come back. That was the way it was with some of the people in the factory especially the ones with learning difficulties, how on earth are these poor men and women going to find work in the current economic environment or more to the point work where they are not going to be exploited and paid a ridiculously low wage.

The manager was doing her best and to be honest under the circumstances she was doing well, I admired her resolve, few new managers would have coped that well I feel. Our customers were understanding of the situation and some had got proposals for taking over the factory, but were selective in who they would keep on, realistically I felt that they were exploiting the situation to get a factory for next to nothing with cheap labour. Thats exactly what I was on about earlier, if our own customers were seizing an opportunity to exploit the situation then what hope is there in the outside world for these people. My management style was to lead by example and to befriend and coax, not wield a stick, this approach suited my character and worked very well. Our new manager was a similar breed but did have the balance sheet as a priority but nevertheless she was a good people person as was the manager before her, believe me that is the exception rather than the norm in The Company.

As weeks turned into Months the time was getting nearer to closure we had all had our individual consultation 1 meeting with a total of two planned, at my individual consultation I informed the interviewers which was the factory manager and an external HR person that I intended to appeal against the redundancy decision and raise a grievance. This would be based merely on the fact that the Company accord which was agreed between The Company and the trade unions and was so heavily relied upon by The Company when it suited them stated that voluntary redundancies would be offered first before compulsory redundancies were imposed. As I applied for voluntary redundancy in 2010 and was turned down as stated in an earlier chapter, I felt I had grounds for the grievance. The terms as one would expect were a lot lower than what was offered in 2010, i.e. In 2010 the offer was one year's salary plus Â£5000. Now it was 3 weeks' pay for every year worked. So the stage is set for yet another grievance.

The unions as one would expect were kicking off all huffing and puffing with no substance, true to form yet another union that was a waste of time and money for that matter. They were going to do this and going to do that but really there going to do nothing except give out a lot of rhetoric.

I decided to fight this one on my own after all I could hardly do a worse job and if I lost well I guess I would still be without a job so I may as well go out guns blazing, The Company wouldn't expect anything less from me and far be it for me to disappoint. It's not that I am constantly looking for trouble although you could be forgiven for thinking that, it's just that I realised after the miners' strike that unions are not what they once were and are only interested in their own political agenda and control in some cases. The only union I felt was half decent was the UDM (union of democratic mineworkers) but as you will no doubt know Neil Greatrex who I had a lot of time for and met personally on a few occasions was not perfect. It is very true of the old adage and I believe it "power corrupts, and absolute power corrupts absolutely". The temptation obviously is too great for some and it is hard to trust. There is corruption everywhere you look and only this week in the news I was listening to how there was corruption in our own government.

Back at the factory the government were inviting a select few to various venues around the country to discuss the redundancy situation, I was one of two chosen at Leicester along with the Unite union rep, and our venue was to be the Ricoh stadium in Coventry. We went along and we had various tables where we sat in groups and each table had a DWP representative there, the main agenda was to brain storm ideas to save The Company, er hang on a minute, the government have decided to withdraw funding now they wanted to find ways of saving it, jeez I'm confused now. One thing that became very apparent though was that everybody was of no doubt that The Company senior directors had mismanaged the Company, but in reality it wasn't rocket science to figure that out. In 2007 the government sent in Price Waterhouse and Cooper to audit the Company and the net result from all that was that the Company was being mismanaged, but guess what nobody lost their cushy number of a job as a result of it. The absolute power analogy again.

At the factory business was as usual or at least on the surface, On one particular Wednesday Leicester College came in as usual to teach life skills to our people this was an invaluable service and the disabled work force got a lot out of it and enjoyed it, I took advantage of this service mainly through discussions with the teachers, I organised the classes and each term I had meetings to discuss the curriculum, it was at one of these meetings where I indicated that I would like to take my maths and English GCSE's or at least the equivalent. They offered to teach me the basics and then take the exams at the end. This resulted in my gaining the qualifications in both Maths and English, At School I would never had attained those qualifications and I was proud of myself for getting them now. Some weeks later I was visited by the education manager and invited to the 2012 Leicester College Awards to Industry Breakfast, I accepted this invitation and attended as requested. It was a very plush event with dignitaries and other Industry representatives, I was absolutely astonished to be announced as the runner up for our category, the college manager told me she nominated me for my dedication to the cause and always finding time to help our people develop themselves. She said she had no input on the award winners only the nomination. I proudly took our certificate back to the factory and showed the manager, she was ecstatic too and said that I had deserved the award, strange thing though was that I didn't think I had done anything to be recognised for but was quietly chuffed anyway.

Back at the factory I was nearing the date for my individual consultation 2 meeting or IC2 as it was known, The Company were holding lots of local team briefs at each factory informing everybody what the latest news was, it didn't seem to matter really because there was no way the outcome was going to be any different, we were all going to be on the dole in less than three months' time. The Manager was doing her best to get everybody's morale up, but she knew she was fighting a losing battle. There were a select few factories that were not going to close until 2013 and those were mainly the factories that had contracts with the automotive industry such as Land Rover, Ford and the like. This was for two reasons mainly one being that to end those contracts early would cost a lot of money and two, was that the factories were earning money and good money in some cases. They were the exception though. The workers at those factories though were worried that they would eventually come under the. TUPE rules which basically means transfer of undertakings whereby if their factory was bought as a going concern they would lose out on the redundancy money.

My day for the IC2 meeting had arrived I chose not to be accompanied by my union rep and to go it alone. In that meeting again was my manager and the external HR guy, they told me that I was confirmed as being made redundant and I would leave the Company on the 28th August. So now it's official and in black and white, in a funny sort of way the realisation was hitting home now, now it was not sometime in the future it is in a few weeks ironically it was to be one week before my eleventh full year at The Company, I mentioned this and said that I would lose one year's redundancy money for the sake of one week. My manager said that the factory would close on the seventh of September my anniversary date was the third of September, she said if I stayed behind to assist her in closing down the site my leaving date would be the seventh of September one week after my anniversary date. I agreed to do that, After-all I was well used to losing out on redundancy packages with the pit and Scottish Power so maybe now at least I can get the full package. I did complain to the HR guy telling him that they should pay for the time worked and to risk losing one year's money for the sake of one week was disgraceful, but nevertheless we had got round that one thanks to my manager.

I have to say that by and large I had enjoyed my time at The Company, sure, I had been through a few disagreements with management but the workforce were marvellous men and women each with personal barriers that they had to live with, they in my view are a credit to us all, never once did I get the disability as an excuse for not doing what was asked. I will miss them all. Maybe in a weird sort of way it will be a good thing, I had for the last few years felt bored and wasted mainly through the lack of progression through the ranks, and I know if I had towed the line and not voiced an opinion I would have progressed a little further through the ranks, the first manager I had at the Leicester factory that I was always locking horns with told me that I would never progress through the ranks because I was too close to the workforce. That could well be true but I had issued disciplinary notices just as much as I had given praise so I can be impartial when the need arises.

I have no regrets for the way I had operated at work, I had my own mind and was quick to voice it at times. There is an old adage that says "to thine own self be true". I believe I have been, I say what I think whether it pleases or offends, before the miner's strike I was not like that at in fact quite the opposite. The miner's strike did toughen me up and that was a positive, that was a big turning point in my life and although I wouldn't say it had scarred me I certainly felt its effects and still to this day I can recall every moment and every emotion that it stirred, so maybe it did scar. I now do what I think or feel to be right and not what everybody wants me to do, tow the party line as it were. If there's a wrong or injustice that affects me or my family, make no mistake I will put it right, another manager of mine at the pit told me that the pen is mightier than the sword and The pen or should I say keyboard nowadays is my weapon of choice and has served me well both in my personal life and in my working life.

My wife Debbie is very supportive and vaguely understands what it must have been like, she is very uncomfortable with all the TV and Radio Interviews though. I am grateful for the interviews and I am eternally grateful to the BBC, They were the only media company that would let me have my say on the reasons for my going back to work. All other mediums were only ever interested in the human impact and the derision between me and my Dad. I have spoken to many people from all over the world such as Hungary, Germany, America and Africa, none of them can understand why the derision has lasted so long. That's just it the proverbial nail on the head, unless you lived it you can never really fully understand. The NUM see me as a traitor, and I see them as having betrayed the trust of the mine workers and denying the fundamental trade union right to a vote. My Dad who has forgiven other miners who broke the strike, told the press that he didn't forgive me because I joined the breakaway Nottinghamshire union the UDM the union of democratic mine workers. Although he contradicts his beliefs because a few of the working miner's he has forgiven were members also. For me though I could not simply carry on paying to a union that not only denies the right to a democratic vote but only wants to oust the government. Like I have said until I am blue in the face, Scargill only ever wanted to parachute into Downing Street and use the power of the miners to do it. Think about this, If he had been successful could any of you really see him giving the miners or any other working groups what they wanted, suppose the miners came to him with a a wage rise in excess of 40% like they did in the seventies, would he pay it? I think not, or at least if he did it would open the flood gates, and before you know it the country is bankrupt. I can hear some of you saying that we are nearly bankrupt now, well, yes, that's true and in my opinion that is directly due to poor government decisions to bail out the bankers, that as we know was Labour, but the Tories are no better either.

Chapter 25

Moving on

It seems that whatever your background and whatever your abilities life will play its part in tripping you up along the journey. I firmly believe that everyone is born equal and we all start out with the same tools. I accept however, that some people are born into a more privileged family and that is of no one's fault either. From my perspective as we now know, I was born into a poor mining family with little or nothing and living hand to mouth day in day out. I did not perform academically at School and always felt that I was out of my depth with Maths, English was a strong point though. I left School at the earliest opportunity with absolutely nothing, I bummed my way through School thinking that I was going down the coal mines for all my working days, maybe this was my first experience of disappointment in the adult world at least.

It would need a damn good Psychologist to fathom my life as it has been written thus far, maybe everybody has a similar tale to tell in some ways. Not everybody has had their working and private lives broadcast to the nation every few years though.

I accept that the playing out of my life and my relationship or lack of with my Father on TV is partly my own doing, at the time I wanted the world to know about the injustice as I saw it of the way Arthur Scargill mismanaged the Miner's strike and cost me my relationship with my Father, this we all know and you must be sick of reading it by now.

After The Company I was determined to turn the sorry experience of redundancy into a positive one, a new chapter if you like, the alternative would be to sit and mope and feel sorry for myself and feeling that yet again I have been stitched up. I have to turn my life round, I have a wife who I love without exception and failing to move on from this would possibly end up with us losing our home, more importantly a home that I did not buy initially, Debbie bought the house from the local authority some years before, in fact ironically around the time of the miner's strike. I simply would not be able to live with the guilt if she lost that through my self-pity.

I always thought that finding work after The Company would be easy, I was to be grossly out of touch with the job market, I applied for literally hundreds of jobs and got rejection after rejection, I was beginning to let the pressure get to me and yes feeling a little sorry for myself, I had to find a decent job before the redundancy money ran out, after all I was going to get no help from the state or anyone else for that matter. It was time now to put that theory to the test, I made the appointment with the local Jobcentre Plus, this was done online and then a telephone call back to confirm the actual time and date.

The day arrived and when I walked into the Jobcentre, there was a security guard there at reception, she asked me if I had an appointment and upon confirming that, I was asked to take a seat. The process I found was a little unnerving and a feeling that I didn't belong there. I waited for what seemed like an age, when I heard my name called out. The lady welcomed me to the Jobcentre which I felt rather strange, who would want to be made welcome in there? I sat down expectantly and listened as she confirmed my details, all was correct, she walked me through the process and told me that I had to apply for at least 10 jobs between the signing days which would be 2 weeks apart. She then asked me if my wife was working, I confirmed this and she then told me that I would receive £71 per week dependent on meeting the criteria with regard to the job applications. I stopped her there and asked her how she knew whether my wife was working full time or part time and how she knew if at all how much money we had coming in. She said that wasn't taken into consideration, if she had a job then that's all that mattered as far as they were concerned. The rest transpired something like this.

JCP rep

"Mr. Whyles, you are only entitled to £71 per week for a maximum of six Months".

ME

"So what happens after the six Months if I am still out of wok then"?

JCP rep

"Nothing that's the end of your benefit entitlement, you will not receive financial support after that time"

ME

"What about my Mortgage? What about income support as it used to be called"?

JCP rep

"As I said Mr. Whyles you will have exhausted your entitlement by then"

During this conversation there was a gentleman at the next desk remonstrating with his advisor (*apparently that's what they are called these days*) saying that he could not survive on £199 per week and they must pay him more. I could tell from his accent that he was eastern European. This enraged me.

ME

"I will have exhausted my entitlement in six Months, I have worked over 30 years without taking a penny from the state in that time and I will have exhausted my entitlement in six Months, What the hell has he contributed to this country"?

JCP rep

"Mr. Whyles you cannot say things like that and if you continue I will have no alternative to have you ejected"

ME

> "Tell you what, shove it where the sun don't shine, he is the reason this country is in the mess it's in".

I got out of my chair to leave as I turned I was met face on with the burly security guard, "Don't worry, I'm leaving" I said.

I headed back home and Debs asked how I got on, from my expression and mutterings, she said "you walked out didn't you".

ME   "Well darling you should have seen it there was this Polish guy kicking off………." Debs butts in.

DEBS "I can imagine the rest", "but you will have to sign on soon because the money is going to run out in the next couple of Months."

ME

> "Yeah I know, but it's so maddening, the whole system is arse over tit"

The reality of course was that if I didn't get work soon I would indeed have to go back and do it all again.

As the next couple of Months came and went without success on the job front, I had to swallow my ego and go back to the JCP.

I made the appointment and just happened to get the same lady at the interview. She was very welcoming and remembered my outburst, merely asking me if I had calmed down a little. I went through the process and I did give her my opinion on the matter but this time in a calm and collected manner or at least outwardly.

So That was it I had to come in the following day to sign on, I did ask why I had to come in again Tomorrow when I was here already but apparently it's based on your NI number. The weeks rolled by and they were ever impressed at the amount of applications I was making, truth is though the more I made the more depressed and feeling worthless I became, I was becoming disheartened at the prospects the future was looking like. Eventually my benefit entitlement ran out and we were living on just Debs wage.

A few weeks later I attended yet another job interview, for a large global company with a branch based in Corby. The interview as all the others I thought went well, the only difference was it was temporary for six Months with no prospects as such of becoming full time, it was a contractor based roll which effectively meant I was self-employed. Normally I wouldn't give it a second look but I'm desperate. I have to pay the Mortgage and in a few weeks' time the money will be all gone. I got home from the interview and had a missed call on the land line phone, I pressed call back it back and it was the agency for the job that I had just been interviewed for, he told me that I had impressed them at the interview and would like to offer the position, the money on offer was a lot less than I had been used to and I knew they were squeezing the limit, but hey, beggars can't be choosers and one has to be in a job to get a job in my opinion.

I have to admit I was feeling better not only about the situation but myself as a man. I started the role on the 7th July 2013, I soon hit it off with my boss and the rest of the team and life was good, the only drawback was to come in November when me and Debs were to go to Gambia as usual for two weeks, this had long been paid for but I would not be getting paid for the holiday, as a self-employed person as some of you will no doubt know, you don't get paid if you are not at work whether that be from holiday, sickness, family emergency…Nothing. This brought it home somewhat, I knew I had to find something else, preferably before the six Months expired.

About this time I received a telephone call from a producer for ITV television telling me that they were producing a programme which would be about the thirtieth anniversary of the 1984 Miner's strike and was I willing to take part. I accepted and they requested contact details for my Dad to ask him if he would take part, I gave the details as requested.

The day of filming arrived and the TV crew turned up at our house to set up the equipment for filming, again Debbie was not comfortable with the media attention but accepted it as she had done many times before. The whole process lasted around five hours with the usual repositioning of furniture and setting up microphone and camera booms etc. My Dad however declined to take part in the filming as he had done on most other occasions. I arranged also to re-visit Colliery Row where I grew up to do some filming there. I was looking forward to this bit as it would be like a look back in time for me and to have it recorded on film was great. During the filming however it was the coldest day I can remember in a long time and several hours standing around waiting for camera crews getting into position and adjusting other equipment made it an extremely cold day, the presence of the camera crew created some interest with the local residents too.

A few weeks after the filming I was contacted by a well-known TV magazine reporter, I was familiar with his name as he was well respected in media circles for his work in the past. He told me that he had received a transcript of the TV programme which was normal practice and would I take part in a feature for the magazine as the subject matter was of great interest to the British public. I agreed and he told me that my Dad had agreed to an interview also. This would be interesting.

The day of the interview arrived and I spent about an hour talking with the reporter, after the interview was concluded, I asked him what my Dad had to say, he sucked his teeth and said that there was one particular comment he made that disturbed him and didn't really want to divulge it. After some persuading from me he said "*Well during the interview your Dad said he was in failing health, to which I asked him that when the time came would he be happy for you to attend his funeral, he responded by saying that he would rather he go to yours.*"

He added after that. "*I can tell by your expression that the comment has hurt you and I am not going to ask you for a response, however he did say that it was a joke but in all honesty I felt he meant it*"

I was hurt as he had quite rightly said, but how does one respond to that, how could he say such a thing to a journalist of all people, had he not learnt anything from his previous remarks that were in a similar vein?

When the reporter left, I was in a blind rage, I telephoned my older Brother Rob, and told him what he had said, he was shocked at the remark but not too surprised, he too had come to expect nothing less from him.

The following week at work I walked into the canteen and some of the guys were reading the magazine, this was identical to the twentieth anniversary at The Company, the same format but a different workforce. As then, the remarks here too were supportive, I was relieved. One guy told me that he didn't agree with my crossing the picket line but the remarks made by my Dad were disgraceful, especially thirty years on.

I eagerly read the article, and felt it was impartial and fair. I now had to wait for the TV programme to air in a couple of Months' time. In the meantime it's just carry on business as usual as it were.

Back at work I did the usual thing by applying for roles, and registering with agencies. As Christmas was approaching, the MD for the Company summoned me and my boss up to his office, I assumed it was to give me my marching orders because the six months would be up at Christmas. Surprisingly he was very impressed with my work as was my boss and offered to extend the contract until February 2014, only 2 Months but another 2 Months that I can pay the Mortgage and look for something else.

The week before Christmas my boss was on holiday and I obviously needed to work as much as possible especially with the prospect of losing another weeks money during the festive period. On the Christmas Eve, The office Manager came to me and gave me a bottle of wine and a Christmas card with a Tesco voucher for £30 in it. I was choked, really choked.

This company was seemingly a good company to work for, the employees were happy and numerous employees said they were paid well. I was undergoing weekly meetings with my boss and the MD by now to see what had been done H&S wise and what needed to be done. These meetings were good and it was always discussed about my longevity with the Company. The MD was trying to get approval to employ me full time, he was a lovely man in a lot of ways and he came across as sincere.

February came and went and by now my contract was literally on a week by week basis, this was not good, I had even less security than before and had to move on before time was called altogether.

The time had arrived now for the airing of the TV programme and it was called "The Miner's Strike and Me". The programme wasn't on until 11pm that was quite late but I had to watch it before going to bed, Debbie had retired earlier. I watched the hour long programme and was somewhat satisfied with how it was portrayed and how I came across, my initial thoughts on seeing the close ups of me was that I looked very old with a few wrinkles showing and I found that quite shocking in some ways.

I was applying for jobs left right and centre, some resulting in interviews and some not. I had one interview for a major car manufacturer in Derby, this I felt that I had no chance of getting as they would want the very best and with uninterrupted experience. I attended the interview with a panel of five of the Management team, it was intensive and I felt uneasy and felt it had not gone that well. At the end of the interview the HR Manager escorted me back to the main entrance where he told me that I had given a good account of myself and that they wold be in touch one way or the other. I felt that he was trying to make me feel better about the expected "On this occasion you have been unsuccessful letter" which usually follows the interviews.

After about a week I was contacted by the employment agency that was dealing with the job for the car manufacturer in Derby, He told me that the team were very impressed with me and would I be able to attend a second interview, he even went so far as to say that I had jumped to the top of the list of favoured candidates as he put it.

I was very surprised at that and was excited to attend a second interview, this was an achievement in itself, and if you get on board with these people then you are at the top of your game professionally.

At the second interview there were just two people, the HR Manager and the production Manager, the interview was a less formal one this time and more relaxed, I was asked questions on my CV (*curriculum Vitae*) especially on dates of employment at different companies. I was asked how I would deal with certain scenarios and how I would deal with people that did not want to conform to Health and Safety rules etc. I answered these just honestly, previously at other interviews I had given answers that I thought they were looking for rather than what I believed. The point they kept bringing up was the point that I lived over fifty miles away and distance had been an issue with former safety officers. I told them that I had always commuted to work around forty miles and used that to prepare myself for the day on the way in and to wind down in the evening on the way home. The interview was concluded and I was told they would be in touch within seven days.

When I got home the agency rang me again saying that the Company had been in touch with them and said that they were very impressed with me and now the role was between me and one other person from an initial one hundred and thirteen people that had applied for the job. It was now as ever just a waiting game, experience had taught me not to get my hopes up but I was quietly excited.

I carried on with my contracted role and was getting ever anxious and excited at the same time about the automotive position. I was constantly telling myself that even if I was unsuccessful again it wasn't down to my lack of expertise or experience.

On the Friday of the following week I received a call as expected from the agency, the agency guy asked me how I was feeling, I told him I felt like an expectant father. He told me that in that case he was about to deliver the baby as the automotive company wanted to offer me the position adding that I was by far and above the best candidate. I could hardly contain my excitement, I accepted the position without delay and was to await for the offer of employment to arrive in the post which I was to sign and return. I did have other irons in the fire as it were but they didn't matter now I had achieved my objective. I was however concerned about the distance as it took an hour and a half to get there and two hours to get back because of traffic congestion.

I formerly accepted the role the following week and had been agreed that I would start in three weeks' time.

When I arrived at work where I was currently working one morning the following week, I had my written termination letter in my hand, but before I had even got to my desk my boss told me that he needed an urgent meeting with me in the board room. I thought this strange as this had never happened previously in the last nine Months. I followed him into the board room. He told me that the MD had decided to extend the current contract until December with a view to making it permanent after that. I obviously at that point told him that the proposition was not acceptable and followed that up by giving him the written termination letter that I had composed. He was shocked to put it mildly, and said he would go upstairs to speak with the MD.

I returned at that point to my desk to continue with my work. I saw the MD several times during the rest of that day and it was obvious that he was ignoring me, it wasn't until the following day when he approached me telling me that he was very angry at my decision to leave but fully understood my reasons for leaving, he then offered his hand, I shook his hand and was feeling a little sorry but sorry doesn't pay the Mortgage and I was doing what was right for me and my family. When my last day arrived I was asked to see the MD, to which I did, he told me that I would be welcome back should things not work out in my new job and that he wanted me to visit the next time I was passing, to which I agreed, I was then presented with a large Easter egg as a leaving gift with a card signed by all the Management team.

At the end of the day I left and promised to keep in touch with my boss which I will do.

Driving home was filled with mixed emotions, I was sorry to be leaving that company but excited to be starting my new job.

CHAPTER 26

The Final Curtain

I soon began fitting in to a new job, the people here were very friendly and professional, my new boss, John was one of the loveliest men I have ever come across either personally or professionally. Within 2 weeks we had a great professional relationship and we had a meeting every Friday afternoon to discuss any issues and my progress etc. He told me that I was a breath of fresh air and that I was everything he expected and more besides. Life here is busy but enjoyable, I had a free hand to prioritise my time and tasks. The only drawback was the distance, it was an issue due to the traffic congestion.

I was issued with a laptop and company phone, this too was a first for me and is where I first started working at home in my own time. However all good things and all that, I had a message on my personal mobile voicemail, It was a Company that I had an interview with some weeks before, they were trying to contact me urgently. I picked up this message on my car phone. When I arrived home I told Debbie that I had a message to call the company, I guessed that they were perhaps wanting to offer me the position I had applied for nearly a Month ago. I was discussing the possibility with Debbie, just as the phone rang again, it was a withheld number so obviously it could be anyone, I answered and it was indeed the HR department for the company in question. She confirmed that they wanted to offer me the position of Health and Safety Officer for two sites in Lincolnshire which were horticultural sites.

I asked if I could mull it over overnight because I had just got settled with my current Company. She agreed and said that the Health and Safety Manager would contact me the following day.

Sure enough the Manager did ring me by which time I had reluctantly decided to accept the position. We agreed that I would start after the Bank holiday Monday which would mean that I would have a full Month's wage from my present job.

That weekend I mulled over the terms and conditions of my current role and it confirmed that in the probationary period I would only need to give one week's notice. I wrote out my notice which took forever, I was wrapped in guilt and feeling that I had let them down badly, I was not the sort to move from job to job at will chasing better terms and conditions. I had two weeks before the bank holiday so that gave me time to receive a written job offer from the new Company before issuing my notice, the whole of the following week was very difficult, I had to play along as it were as if nothing had changed, on the Friday I had the weekly meeting with the HR Manager as normal and he was telling me that he had now relaxed and was sure I was here for the long term and at last he could let go of the reins and let me manage it. That hit me hard like a sledge hammer, I knew all along that come Monday Morning I would be handing in my notice.

The whole weekend I didn't rest easy with my conscience not so much that I was throwing away a good job with a major car manufacturer that most people would give their right arm for, but the fact that I was letting a man down who I had immense respect and admiration for, he firmly believed in me and had placed his trust in me. I was about to throw it all in his face, I am simply not looking forward to Monday.

So the weekend past and it was just as restless as expected. I saw my boss as soon as I arrived at the office, he was sat at his desk which is situated next to mine.

HR Manager
"Good Morning Steve, I trust you had a good weekend?"

ME
"Well not exactly"

HR manager
"Oh, is it something I can help you with?"

ME
"Not exactly but I do need a meeting first thing today"

HR Manager
"Ok, boardroom four is free we can go in there now, let's get a coffee and shut ourselves in there."

We went into the boardroom via the coffee machine and I told him I was leaving, handing him the letter.

He was devastated, I could see that, but being the true gentleman that he is never vented any anger, just a solemn expression. He told me that he needed to see the MD and that he would call me back later in the day, he asked me if I would work the weeks' notice, to which I confirmed I would do. I resumed my job as if everything was normal, it was like a false reality if that makes sense, My boss throughout the day was no different to how he was normally, he was indeed a true professional, if I had stayed I would have learned a lot from him I have no doubts about that.

The days went by as normal until I arrived on the Friday my last day. My boss said he would meet me at 4pm for an exit interview.

I worked the day as normal and went to the boardroom at 4pm where he joined me. We discussed the reasons for my leaving, he asked me if there was anything that would change my mind, he offered more money and less hours, but in reality he could not offer a shorter commute which was the only reason for leaving.

He told me that he would like to keep in touch and would like me to take advantage of his holiday home that he owned in the Cameroon.

He asked if I would be willing to help them out with the health and safety on a part time basis such as evenings and weekends, he had discussed this with the MD and they would be happy for me to remain on the books as a consultant. I agreed to this and felt that it was the least I could do for them after letting them down.

I left the Company on friendly terms and I remain in contact with them to this day. The part time working never transpired, so it has fallen back into the HR Manager's remit.

***

So here I was again leaving one Company with sadness and looking forward to be starting with a new one the following week.

I started the with my new job as planned after the bank holiday, this was to be an entirely different experience, managing the Health and Safety of two large Horticultural nurseries was going to be a challenge. A challenge that I relished.

A couple of weeks into the job I was just getting into my car to come home when my phone beeped telling me that I had a voicemail, as my car was connected to my phone by Bluetooth I spoke to the car to tell the system to ring voice mail. I began my journey whilst the car connected and the voicemail was from my Sister Rachel, she said to ring her as soon as I got the message.

I knew that it had to be either something to do with my Mother or Father, it had to be. I pulled over into a layby and took the phone off the cradle and preceded to call her back, it was then that I noticed that there were 3 missed calls.

She answered the phone and I asked her if she was ok, she said she wasn't, and then told me that my Dad had passed away earlier that Morning. She went on to say how at the weekend he was talking about how he was 78 years old and that he had a good innings, as if he knew. And he died two days later suddenly with no apparent illness, he had survived four heart attacks in the last thirty years the first one when he was 44 years old.

Well the news stunned me, part of me was deeply saddened and the other part resentful that if he was sure he was going to die soon, he never contemplated one bit about us getting together and discussing our differences, Yes I loved him, Yes I am disappointed with him, and Yes I feel betrayed in some ways that he didn't do that. It tells me that everything he said about me such as calling me a scab on his deathbed, and wanting to go to my Funeral first, he obviously meant. The fact of the matter is, in all reality is that he had three sons and one daughter, he has only ever had a relationship with his Daughter my sister in the previous Ten to thirty Years, he obviously disowned me Thirty years ago my oldest Brother Rob was disowned after a fall out between them Twenty years ago and my youngest Brother David has not been in contact with him in the last Ten Years. I can't in all honesty feel that I will miss him as such, I lost him Thirty Years ago in effect and I suppose I went through all the emotions of that then, now I feel some resentment at him passing away without us thrashing this out. In public at family events associated with my Sister such as her Wedding and the Christening of her Daughter he was always friendly and took time to make conversation albeit small talk, but talk nonetheless. Latterly at my Uncle Alan's funeral he even sat with me and Debbie at the wake, so those events were what kept the spark alight in some ways, only now I realise that it was all a show for public perception. My Sister had told me that she would let me know when the funeral was, I told her to contact me should there be anything I could do to help her. My Mother has Alzheimer's and is not really with it.

Due to my Dads specific instructions the funeral could not take place as would be normal as he had wanted a certain funeral director to deal with the arrangements and he was on holiday so things would be put on hold for a little while.

It was to be a week or so later when I was contacted by 3 journalists from 3 different newspapers asking me if I would be attending my Father's funeral and what my initial thoughts were. I was incensed at this, I told the first reporter that I was not going to comment on that and as far as the funeral is concerned we don't know when that is as yet. The reporter to my astonishment told me what day and time the funeral was and that it had appeared in the local paper, three days ago. Obviously this made an issue because I had not been contacted by my Sister as she had promised to do to tell me that, in fact only a few days before I texted her to see if she was ok and if there was any news. She answered saying she was bearing up and there were still no news, obviously this was not the case as she was the one that had made the announcement in the local paper. I being over Fifty miles away do not receive or have access to that paper. I cannot help but feel that my Mother had something to do with that, Alzheimer's or not.

So to round up, I feel that the legacy of the mine's strike and the derision it caused between me and my Dad is over, but only because he passed away. It is ironic that for the last 30 years I never believed that he truly believed what he was portraying in his outbursts to the media. Only after his passing was it clear to me without any shadow of doubt that he truly did believe it. My overall opinion of my Father has changed and for the first time in the whole saga I am filled with contempt for him, he firmly believed that he would be leaving this world in a very short time and he chose to meet his maker without so much as a regret of any description.

If it had not been for his willingness to put aside our differences at family events then I would have understood his reluctance to end the feud. He could apparently switch it on and off at will but not when it really mattered. So my summary is that I thank my dad for the Twenty years of love and good fathering before the strike and I am truly sorry that he felt that he was not strong enough to allow blood to be thicker than water. I can fully understand his disappointment and embarrassment perhaps of my breaking the 1984-85 Miner's strike but if he was a real man and half the man I thought he was then he should have done the right thing after a few Months. I said earlier in this book that the Whyles family were notorious for their stubbornness and reluctance to forgive, I am just as stubborn in a lot of ways but My Dad had allowed that stubbornness to consume his life. He openly forgave other people who he had no paternal ties with who did the exact same thing as I did, yet he could not and would not do what any decent father would do and that is to forgive, maybe not forget but forgive his own Son. It may sound like I feel as though I am guilty of something, the truth is I don't feel I did anything in 1984 to be forgiven for. I have closed many an interview with the following statement and I will close this book in the same way.

> "I have one regret, and it is the only regret and that is the family break up. As for everything else I would do it all again tomorrow."

END NOTE
Britain's greatest escape

In this the final chapter, I will if I may go on some more about Arthur Scargill. I think it important to express to the public just how lucky we all were that Arthur Scargill did not succeed in overthrowing the conservative government, After reading the following paragraphs of actual comments made by him in TV, radio and newspaper interviews, you will I hope just realize what a lucky escape this country had in 1984-1985.

At a speech at Sherwood in Mansfield on the 12th November 1981 Arthur Scargill said "*I believe it is in the long term interests of the miner's to have a strong, vigorous and democratic union which responds effectively and quickly to the wishes of the members"*. Oh really, where was the democratic right to a national ballot then in 1984?

In a reply to Mr. Ken Toon's support for a national ballot, Arthur Scargill said in the Times newspaper on the 15th April 1984 *"I shall have to rule out of order a resolution which need not be put."* How can that be out of order in a democracy?

In The Marxism Today in April 1981 Arthur Scargill said when asked about workers having control. *"I disagree totally and utterly with the concept of workers' control....It is only by politicizing our membership that we will ever bring about the underline shift towards a socialist system in society. Therefore I don't agree that we ought to be putting workers on the boards, I am against the whole concept of participation which only serves to perpetuate the capitalist system."*

You will note that I have underlined the word irreversible, this is very significant, and it means that when socialism has its grip and communism or moreover Stalinism is in power, all rights to ballots and elections will be ruled out and enforced, Irreversible means no going back does it not?

An article in the Daily Telegraph in May 1981 remarks were made against Scargill, The trade union movement and Tony Benn, Scargill said at an address to a meeting in Easington, Co. Durham. *"There are union members in the media, and I hope they remember that if they didn't write this filth, it wouldn't get printed, and if the printing unions didn't print it, we wouldn't have to read it"* Absolutely laughable but again an indicator as to how freedom of speech and the press would be quelled under a socialist Britain.

Scargill was reported to say at a rally in the Guardian in September 1982 that he would nationalize the TV, Radio and press in an instant, we already know that nationalization means control and denial to the public in a socialist Britain.

Proof if proof were needed of an impending dictatorship under Scargill and Stalinism was in 1975 when he said

"The ideal way that the working class can achieve working class power, is through the election of a Labour Government controlled by the Left Marxist Groups, which should be admitted to the Labour Party. The Labour Government should in turn be committed to accept conference decisions that are controlled by the Trade Union block vote, you can then win the positions which are necessary to change society. The reformist democratic Labour Party will then have completely served its purpose, and no doubt elections could then be scrapped and the dictatorship of totalitarian socialism be brought in." I know you will probably have read that twice to double check that what you thought it said was actually said, guess what, you read it right first time.

In 1975 Scargill said in The New Left Review.

*"I want to take into common ownership everything in Britain,
we could take over all the means of production, distribution and
exchange more or less immediately."*

Scargill and his scaremongering and manipulation of the truth to further his own ends and to court favour from the Miner's

There are some major allegations that I recall from my notes for prosperity, these are set out below with the correct facts.

The Coal Board wants to butcher the coal industry, because Ian Macgregor announced a drop of 8.5 million tons from 1984, as a result of which 40,000 jobs would be lost. The fact is that planned reduction was about 4 million tons, manpower would be reduced by 20,000. Scargill manipulated the truth and doubled the figures.

Pit closures will throw thousands of miners' on the scrap heap. The true fact is that the coal board would avoid compulsory redundancies, furthermore anyone who wished to stay in the coal industry would be offered another job in it. The terms offered would be the best terms ever offered to British workers.

I think it is fair to say that I have proved my case against Arthur Scargill, I have proved that his only reason for bringing the Miner's out on strike in 1984 was not to protest against pit closures but to simply use the miner's to bring this country to its knees, he had no interest in the interests of the miner's he was ever only interested in using us the miner's to help establish a communist state, then discard them, he admitted above that he didn't trust the miner's, and that was why he would not want them to share the power he so desperately craved for.

Arthur Scargill made visits to Cuba and Russia to secure funding and support, and under a pseudonym need I remind you that both of these countries are communist.

As I said earlier if he was really interested in fighting for the coal mines he would have given the Miner's a national ballot, a ballot was the only way he could ever have hoped to get the support of other unions, and I firmly believe that a ballot would have been against Strike action. I repeat to Mr. Scargill that the only way to keep pits open is through the pick and shovel and not the axe and sickle. You simply cannot abandon a coal mine for twelve Months and expect to carry on from where you left off.

Say of Mrs. Thatcher what you will, I for one although not a supporter of her policies admired the grit and determination that that she showed in 1984-1985 had she had buckled under the weight of heavy communism then Britain today I have no doubt would be a very different and scary place to live in.

"The writing of this book has been a journey of mixed emotions, numerous people have said that I should

Write a book, and here it is. It has stirred many memories in the writing, some memorable, some I would

Rather have forgotten, It has evoked tears of laughter and tears of pain, some parts were easy to write and

Some were difficult to both write and recall. I hope that along the journey you have taken through this book

I have given you some insight along with a little sadness but some laughter too, if that is the case then the

Book has achieved its goal."

I would like to dedicate this book to my loving Wife Debbie, and my Daughter Maria without their support this book would not have been possible. They have taken part of this journey with me and have seen, witnessed and above all supported me and helped me with the ups and downs of my emotions when recalling difficult parts of my life. All I can say to Debbie is "I love you more today than yesterday but not as much as tomorrow," For Maria my Daughter, No Father has a greater love or pride for his daughter than I do for you, you think only of others and rarely of yourself and are an amazing Mother to our Grand Children. I love you all xx.

Printed in Great Britain
by Amazon.co.uk, Ltd.,
Marston Gate.